THE MEDIUM WHO BAFFLED HOUDINI
MARGERY CRANDON

BOSTON MEDIUM BAFFLES EXPERTS.
HOUDINI THE MAGICIAN STUMPED!

ELAINE M. KUZMESKUS

Copyright by Elaine M. Kuzmeskus, 2015.

Disclaimer:

Publisher disclaim any liability or responsibility for the author's statements, words, ideas, criticisms or observations, and assumes no responsibility for errors, inaccuracies, or omissions.

No part of this book may be reproduced, copied or used in any form or manner whatsoever without written permission, except in the case of brief quotations in reviews and critical articles.

Published by Aventine Press
55 East Emerson St.
Chula Vista CA 91911
www.aventinepress.com

ISBN: 978-1-59330-883-4

Printed in the United States of America
All rights reserved.

Acknowledgements

This book began as a quest learn more about the last of the great physical mediums, Margery Crandon. The manuscript has been revised twice. I would like to acknowledge Susan Roberts for her initial edit. Her enthusiasm and encouragement helped to keep me on track. The final edit was done by Roberta Buland of Right Words Unlimited. Her extensive editing eliminated clichés and careless errors, and gave the book its professional polish. Both editors had a unique sensitivity to Margery Crandon's spell-binding story. I feel fortunate to have worked with these talented professionals.

Dedication

This book is dedicated to the Cabinet Group at the New England School of Metaphysics. May Margery Crandon's courage, ingenuity, and superb physical mediumship inspire you in your quest for physical evidence to prove the continuity of life. No matter how difficult the task, skeptical the scientist, or complex the experiment, she cheerfully complied with her researcher's requests. Margery Crandon truly was the last of the great physical mediums.

Reviews of Books by Elaine Kuzmeskus

Séance 101: Physical Mediumship
Review by Raul Dasilva, January 27, 2008

This work is not to be taken lightly. It was written by an educated and skilled practitioner not just a researcher. As in the case of more prominent mediums (e.g. as in the media) such as John Edwards and James Van Praagh Elaine Kuzmeskus was born with the gift of discernment beyond the sensory levels of perception. However unlike many mediums we're heard about from as far back as the 19th Century she is educated and approaches the subject using the empirical system of scientific inquiry.

The book is filled with much data on the practice and includes a comprehensive review of physical mediumship as practiced by well-known mediums and on up to individuals such as Sathya Sai Baba who is renown through India as an Avatar.

Thankfully, this book is not a tome of tiresome anecdotal verbiage but an in-depth review at what I call the emerging consciousness of multi-dimensional existence in the progress of the human condition. It's read in two or three easy sittings replete with a glossary and endnotes or index: highly recommended.

The Art of Mediumship
Review by Ann McGuffy, December 13, 2012

The Art of Mediumship Elaine Kuzmeskus, MS, is a well-known Medium. She has conducted many séances, presentations, and consultations regarding the supernatural world and the paranormal. She is nationally recognized as a Spiritualist. In this book, Elaine details the history of "Mediumship", explaining what it is and how it works. She also explains how one can develop their gifts and skills. In one chapter, Elaine balances science with the Afterlife, going into the "natural law" of each. The book is very detailed in its research and explanations, particularly of "Mediumship." She also discusses

Spiritual Guides, other types of "guides", psychic detectives, and medical clairvoyants. There are many illustrations, photos, resources, a glossary, and notes to support her information. Whether you believe or not is your choice, but this is a very fascinating book, regardless.

The Making of a Medium
Review by Stephen A. Hermann on March 30, 2013

A GREAT Book by a GREAT Medium!

This book is completely superior to most of the mass- produced autobiographies of mediums that are usually written by ghost writers. Elaine is a very talented medium and an excellent teacher. Compared to many of the popular mediums, made famous through publicists and media hype, Elaine possesses expertise gained through decades of serious study and experience. This book might not be slick like a Hay House publication but anyone interested in the development of mediumship will learn much from reading this book. As a professional medium myself I have great respect for Elaine as a medium and teacher of psychic development. Over the years I have told many people in her area to attend her classes or have private sessions with her. Read this book as it will greatly increase your awareness of the spirit world and the process of mediumistic unfoldment.

Table Of Contents

1	The Medium Who Baffled Houdini	1
2	Too Attractive for Her Own Good	7
3	Boston, 1923	13
4	It All Started as a Lark	19
5	Table Tipping and All That Jazz	23
6	Margery the Medium	29
7	Phenomena and More Phenomena	37
8	Scientific American Committee	45
9	Enter Harry Houdini	53
10	Magician Meets Medium	61
11	Walter Versus Houdini	75
12	"J.B. Rhine is an Ass"	81
13	Harvard University Investigates	91
14	American Society for Psychic Research, Part I	97
15	Case For and Against Psychical Belief	105
16	Margery in Winnipeg, Canada	113
17	ASPR: Margery Mediumship Part II	119
18	Psychic Photography	125
19	Linking Wooden Rings and Cross Correspondences	131
20	Backlash	139
21	"Spooky Fingerprints"	145
22	"You'll Always Be Guessing"	151
Index		155

Chapter 1

The Medium Who Baffled Houdini

Sir Oliver Lodge, Sir Arthur Conan Doyle believed in her; Harry Houdini offered $5,000 to charity if she produced any "manifestations" which he could not duplicate. **Time Magazine**

"Boston Medium Baffles Experts," proclaimed the *Boston Herald* newspaper in 1924. Later headlines read "Houdini the Magician Stumped."[1] Who was this medium who baffled Houdini? She was none other than Margery Crandon the thirty-six- year- old wife of a prominent Boston surgeon. Dubbed "the blonde witch" by the press, Mrs. Crandon continued to captivate the public throughout the 1920s.

While no longer in the public eye, Margery Crandon's death was noted in *Time Magazine's* milestones for the week of November 10, 1941. Her obituary appeared just above that of Simon Guggenheim, who in 1925 established the John Simon Guggenheim Memorial Foundation with a $3,000,000 donation. Margery Crandon had gladly given in the 1920s as well. When "Scientific American" magazine offered a $2,500 prize to the first medium who could produce "conclusive psychic manifestations" under test conditions, Margery Crandon accepted the challenge, and should she win, planned to decline the prize money.

She was as generous as Simon Guggenheim. However, life in the séance room was not as kind to her as the mining industry had been to the wealthy philanthropist who died at age seventy-three from pneumonia. When Margery, fifty-three, slipped from the bonds of earth, it was after years of alcoholism- a fact mercifully omitted from her obituary:

Died. Mina Stinson Crandon, 53, better known as "Margery" the medium whose claims of psychic communication with the dead raised serious controversy from 1924 to 1935; in Boston. Sir Oliver Lodge, Sir Arthur Conan Doyle believed in her; Harry Houdini offered $5,000 to charity if she produced any "manifestations" which he could not duplicate. Charity never got the money.[2]

1

The Medium Who Baffled Houdini

At the time of her death Margery Crandon had outlived her most severe critic, magician Harry Houdini, who died on October 31, 1926, as well as her staunchest supporter, Sir Arthur Conan Doyle, who passed to the other side on July 7, 1930. Both men had been friends before they met the medium. In fact, it was Spiritualist Doyle's support of Margery Crandon that led to the breakup of his friendship with Houdini. It was probably inevitable, that the two would part because Doyle was a Spiritualist, while Houdini detested psychics and had even written *A Magician Among the Spirits*, a book critical of mediums.

Margery Crandon also outlived her other fans- working folks who earned $15 a week. They eagerly looked forward to each installment of the Beacon Hill medium's adventure in the séance room. Later, those who cheered would be just as quick to turn their backs as Margery's séances came under a cloud of suspicion. However, at the height of her fame, Margery the Medium, could do no wrong. She garnered her share of attention in Boston and New York. The public loved to read how "Margery, Boston Medium, Passes all Psychic Tests." Her fans felt triumphant at the sight of headline: "Houdini the Magician Stumped." [3]

Houdini was not the only one fascinated. American researchers Dr. Walter F. Prince, Dr. D. F. Comstock, Dr. William McDougall, along with Britain's Hereward Carrington investigated Margery Crandon's mediumship. Arthur Findlay and Sir Arthur Conan Doyle even crossed the Atlantic to attend her Boston séances. Findlay was so impressed, he proclaimed Margery "the eighth wonder of the world." Sir Arthur Conan Doyle, equally smitten, submitted her name to *Scientific American*. The magazine was eager to investigate psychic phenomena with the latest of scientific equipment.

The committee also researched other mediums- Josie K. Stewart; Juliana Thompson, a noted British trance medium; and George Valiantine, a well-known New York medium. Josie K Stewart was quickly eliminated. George Valiantine was considered the most serious contender, as Juliana Thompson had been found untrustworthy by Dr. Richard Hodgson, years before. [4]

Valiantine, however, was quickly ruled out when Malcolm Bird pointed out an "examination of the trumpet developed the facts that it was quite warm at the point where a human hand would naturally and conveniently grasp it, and that the mouthpiece was damp." [5]

With the spotlight solely on Margery Crandon, she made even more headlines. *The Boston Herald* proclaimed "Scientists Find No Trickery in a Score of Séances" After over forty sittings, the Scientific American committee was just about to award Margery Crandon its $2,500 prize for genuine mediumship when magician, Harry Houdini stepped in. Headlines now ran "Houdini the Magician Stumped." It would take some doing for Houdini to corner Margery.

At first, the medium and magician were cordial to each other. Walter, Margery's spirit control, was not as warm. During the first séance, Walter asked Houdini, "Where would you like the trumpet?" Houdini yelled, "Over here." The trumpet which usually floated easily through the air above the sitters, abruptly made a nosedive for Houdini's feet. At a later séance, Walter became incensed when someone tried to plant a ruler in his sister's séance cabinet.

Walter blurted out, "Houdini, get out of there and never come back. If you don't, I will!"6 Houdini, at that point, became enemy number one. The Crandons, though civil, were no longer cordial. Houdini was so vexed by the medium that he returned from a trip abroad just to cast a dissenting vote when he heard that the Scientific American committee was leaning toward a positive vote.

Immediately, Houdini began a one-man crusade against Margery Crandon. What did the other members of the committee have to say? Hereward Carrington, one of England's most experienced psychic investigators, defended the medium: "As a result of more than forty sittings with Margery, I have arrived at the definite conclusion that genuine supernormal phenomena frequently occur." However, other members who first believed in Margery Crandon, began to have their doubts. In the end, members of the Boston Society for Psychical Research (B.S.P.R.) split in their opinion of the authenticity of the physical phenomena produced by Margery Crandon. The B.S.P.R. became so evenly divided that it eventually disbanded.

Who was this extraordinary woman? First, she was a sister, wife and mother- roles common of many woman. However, during the Roaring Twenties the rules for women were changing. Not only did they have the vote, but they also shortened their skirts. The Twenties represented freedom to women, along with bobbed hair and jazz. By the time the

Twenties were in full swing, Margery had divorced a bullish grocer, John Rand. When she married for a second time, the ex-Mrs. Rand "traded up."

Her second husband, Dr. Le Roi Crandon, was a Mayflower descendent. Of course, being a third wife could have some financial drawbacks. However, no one would have guessed from all outward appearances. The middle-aged physician with his beautiful young bride beaming at his side made the perfect Beacon Hill couple. Dr. Crandon even adopted Margery's young son, John.

Their congeniality only increased when Dr. Crandon, an avid reader of parapsychology literature discovered his young wife's psychic ability. She became the perfect medium. Her mediumship progressed rapidly from table-tilting to trance mediumship and finally trumpet séances which included apports, materialized objects. It wasn't long before Dr. Crandon's gifted wife was creating a stir in Boston's elite drawing rooms as well as the séance room on the third floor of their posh Beacon Hill home. Not every guest approved of the hostess. Some claimed Mrs. Crandon was "too attractive for her own good."

Fortunately, Margery was never one to be bothered by public opinion. However, Dr. Crandon had his reputation as a surgeon to consider, so the couple kept Margery's mediumship "hush hush." While the doctor readily agreed to *Scientific American* editor, J. Malcolm Bird's request to write a book on his wife's physical mediumship, it was with the stipulation that her real name "Mina Crandon" would not be revealed. Bird then suggested the name "Margery" as a cover and referred to Dr. Crandon as F.H., short for "Friend Husband" in his book, *Margery the Medium*. With all the publicity the book generated, it wasn't long before reporters sniffed out the true identity of Margery the Medium, that she was none other than Mina Crandon, the wife of Dr. Le Roi Crandon. This disclosure only served to whet the public's appetite for more of Margery's exploits. By the mid 1924 Margery Crandon not only made headlines in Boston but also across the United States.

Why not? Margery Crandon did it all. The trance medium produced spirit writing, psychic music, voices of the dead through trumpets, and even apports. Unlike the spirit chitchat of tea-room readers, her astonishing array of psychic phenomena was validated by Harvard scientists.

Margery Crandon readily submitted to scientific test after test. Eventually her mediumship would fill two volumes for the American Society for Psychical Research. It was no wonder that psychic researchers considered Margery Crandon to be the greatest medium of her day.

However, even great mediums have been known to cheat. For instance, Italian cabinet medium, Eusapia Palladino, who levitated tables, produced raps and music all while tied up inside her cabinet was caught cheating. Researchers at Cambridge spied her trying to get her leg back into the cabinet and moved its contents about. In the end, the Palladino committee became convinced that, in spite of this fraud, there was some truth to her mediumship:

"It was only through constant repetition of the same phenomenon in a good fight and at moments when its occurrence was expected and after finding that none of the precautions which we took had any influence in impeding it, that we gradually reached the conviction that some force was in play which was beyond the reach of ordinary control and beyond the skill of the most skillful conjurer."[7]

Even Eusapia Palladino was declared to be fraudulent. However, it is hard to imagine how any medium could get away with trickery under such strict conditions as improvised by the Harvard scientists--let alone forty times. No, there had to be more to Margery Crandon's mediumship than the sleight of hand suggested by Harry Houdini.

One cannot help but speculate "Were there really supernatural forces at work?" or "Was it for secondary gain?" As the wife of a wealthy Boston surgeon, Margery Crandon had no need for payment for her work. As for fame, the Crandons had more to lose than gain by publicity. If there was a secondary gain for Medium Margery, it would be to please her husband who was more interested in psychic phenomena. Margery, in the beginning at least, did not feel she had any special abilities. She even laughed at the thought when a tea room psychic said she had the gift. She only agreed to be part of her husband's table- tipping experiment to make Dr. Crandon happy. No one was more surprised when the spirits indicated she was a physical medium.

It wasn't long before Margery shared her husband's enthusiasm. She progressed with amazing speed from table-tipping to deep trance and finally trumpet séances. Here raps, breezes, lights and the distinct voice of her deceased brother came through the trumpet. While some suspected trickery, Margery Crandon was never found wanting under the keen eyes of Harvard scientists. She submitted to test after test- the glass cabinet, the Voice Out Machine--specifically devised to rule out deception.

Why then did her powers fail her in the end? Even her supporters were baffled when a set of fingerprints purported to be from a spirit turned out to be those of her dentist, though other spirit prints had been judged genuine by experts. With so much investigation- two volumes in *American Society for Psychical Research* alone; a 518 page book, *Margery the Medium*, and scores of articles in *Time*, *Scientific American*, and other leading publications-- the medium left the experts scratching their heads. If Margery Crandon had been granted a final headline, it would have to be "Boston Medium Still Baffles Experts."

End Notes

1. http://www.fst.org/margery.htm.
2. *Time Magazine,*" Milestones, November 10, 1941."
3. http://www.fst.org/margery.htm.
4. http://www.survivalafterdeath.org/mediums/thompson.htm.
5. http://www.survivalafterdeath.org/mediums/valiantine.htm.6. http://www.fst.org/margery.htmMina.
7. http://www.survivalafterdeath.org/articles/tyrrell/fraud.htmPhysical Mediumship: Is there Anything Besides Fraud in the Physical Séance?

Chapter 2

Too Attractive for Her Own Good

Margery's best friends were her worst enemies.[1] **Eileen Garrett**

Margery Crandon was born Mina Stinson in 1888 on a farm in Princeton Ontario, Canada- not far from the capital, Toronto. Like the early Ontario settlers who established trading posts on Hudson Bay, Mina's parents were hard working. Mina was the last of the Stinson's six children. At that time, Ontario vied with Quebec in terms of growth in population, industry, arts, and communications- with one important difference. While French was spoken in Catholic Quebec, English was the language of Protestant Ontario. During Mina's childhood, Ontario was largely agricultural. It wasn't until 1904 that the Ford Motor Company came into the area. From all accounts, she had a good upbringing. Mother Stinson openly lavished affection on her baby, in contrast to Mr. Stinson's stoic undemonstrative approach to child-rearing.

The slender, blonde daughter with sparkling blue eyes was fun-loving like her mother. Mina loved to roam the farm, sharing adventures with her brother Walter, who was five years her senior. Before Walter left the farm, he also shared his psychic exploits with "the kid," including table-tipping. The practice was simple enough. The two simply placed their hands lightly on a table and waited for the spirits to move or rap on the table. Table- tilting had become the rage ever since Kate and Maggie Fox had demonstrated their abilities to communicate with spirits by means of raps.

On March 31, 1848, Maggie who was fifteen and her twelve-year-old sister, Kate, began to hear rapping sounds in the basement of their home in the hamlet of Hydesville, New York. When they told their mother, Mrs. Fox, she was convinced that their farmhouse was haunted. However, her husband, John, the local blacksmith, was skeptical. After all, the sounds could be just a loose board. The sisters insisted that the raps came from a spirit that they dubbed "Mr. Splitfoot." They soon devised a simple code- one rap for no, two raps for yes, and three raps for maybe. Later, they laboriously and accurately decoded the names of the deceased through a series of raps one rap for A, two raps for B, three raps for C, and so forth. It wasn't long before the Fox sister were demonstrating their mediumship on stage at Corinthian Hall in nearby Rochester, New York.

Table-tipping soon became the rage in Victorian drawing rooms across America. Spiritualist mediums and believers such as Harriet Beecher Stowe and her sister, Isabella Beecher Hooker, indulged in table-tipping. Even Mary Todd Lincoln invited Hartford medium, Nettie Colburn, to the White House. It wasn't long before the fad spread to England and Canada. Walter Stinson was one of those who took an interest in table-tipping. Whether he was able to contact the spirits through table-tipping is not known. What is known is that "Walter Stinson in his youth had "tables tilt, and levitate in his presence in day light."[2] Walter viewed table tipping as a diversion not to be taken seriously. However, there were times when a table shook so violently that is was completely demolished much to his father's consternation.

Father Stinson disapproved of this ungodly practice. In the world of the turn of the century farmer, a father's admonishments were taken seriously. It was not that women didn't play a vital role on the farm. Mother Stinson, under her husband's authority, most likely had a list of daily chores for her children to do. If a farm were to prosper, everyone had to pitch in. When a farm failed, it spelled disaster for the whole family as there was no socialized medicine or Social Security in Canada in the early 1900s. Everyone worked hard. Father Stinson believed "Idle hands are the work of the devil."

As soon as he came of age, Walter decided to strike out on this own. He craved more adventure than the annual plowing match or country fair. While he enjoyed the simple pleasures of apple pies, folk music, and pitching horseshoes, he was rebellious and wanted to work on the railroad in Boston. It turned out to be an unfortunate choice. In 1911, at the age of twenty eight, he was killed when a boxcar overturned and crushed him.

When Mina completed high school "in good standing,"[3] she followed her brother to the big city where she found a job as a secretary at the

Union Congregational Church, a suitable job for a young woman. The attractive, outgoing beauty quickly became known for her good humor and musical ability. During her teen years, she had played in local orchestras and now, Mina, an accomplished cello player, played in the church orchestra. Soon she caught the eye of one of the parishioners, Earl Rand. The couple married on September 5 1910, and had a son, John, in 1913.

Usually the birth of a child strengthens the bond between a married couple. However, it can weaken an already flawed partnership. The child in such a bond becomes part of a triangle--often to the detriment of the marriage bond. After John was born, Mina wanted more for her son. She was quickly becoming bored as the wife of a small-time grocer. By 1913 she was pondering her options- a marriage without love or divorce.

While marriage did not suit Mina, neither did the prospect of a divorce- an unthinkable choice for a respectable woman in1913. "No," thought Mina, "divorce is out of the question. Once you make your bed you have to lie in it." However, the vivacious young mother had no qualms about taking on a job. Soon she was spending more time out the house. She had volunteered of all things to drive an ambulance. Earl, who was against the idea of Mrs. Rand driving anything let alone an ambulance, eventually gave into his willful wife. Besides, with a young son at home, he didn't want any trouble in the house. The young husband tried to console himself with the thought "Plenty of woman were driving ambulances to help out in the war." Still neighbors heard the loud arguments from the Rand apartment.

If Mina emerged the next day with bruises on her arms, no one asked any questions. Decent folks simply kept such things to themselves. While most husbands didn't engage in wife beating, those who did had little fear of the law. If a bruised wife dared to file a report against her husband, she would receive very little sympathy. "You married him, lady," a blue-uniformed Boston policeman would scold her, thus closing the case.

In a working class neighborhood in which the Rands lived, a divorce was not an option. Sure, some loafers walked out, but women always stayed for the family. For all his troubles, Earl was not about to leave. His family had a small grocery business at Faneuil Hall and were respectable people.

No, Earl Rand really needn't concern himself about his wife's bruises. It was not that wife beating wasn't against the law. Even the Puritans forbade it. "No man shall strike his wife nor any woman strike her husband on penalty of such fine not exceeding ten pounds for one offense, or such corporal punishment as the County shall determine."[4] It was a law that was simply ignored. By Victorian times wife beating was so rampant that when the Women's Rights Convention convened in 1848 at Seneca Falls, New York, they chose to examine the husband's right to chastise his wife as their first order of business.

Hardly a liberated woman, Mina Rand was still headstrong. By the end of 1917, she had put up with Earl's tirades and abuse long enough. On Christmas Day, she fled to her mother's house in Belmont, Massachusetts, with her five-year-old-son in tow. When she left, Mina had no intentions of returning to Earl Rand, his family, or the nosey neighbors. On January 18, 1918, she filed for divorce citing her husband with "cruel and abusive treatment."

It was a case of the carrot and the stick. If Earl Rand represented the stick, Dr. Le Roi Crandon was the carrot. Mina Rand had fallen in love with the tall, serious man fourteen years her senior. Dr. Crandon was Boston Brahmin. "In North America a Brahmin is also a member of the blue-blooded class of New Englanders who claim hereditary or cultural descent from the original Anglo-Saxon Protestants who founded the city of Boston, Massachusetts."[5] An instructor of surgery at Harvard University, he offered Mina a life well beyond her farm girl fantasies. That included a posh home on Beacon Hill, fawning servants, high social status and security. "Plus," as Mina told her friends who cautioned her on the match, "he is crazy about the kid. He plans to adopt John."

It was not that Mina had much to be worry about. She had liked Dr. Crandon from the start. The two first met when he was her surgeon. Although it was strictly professional, still he was most attentive. Later, they met again when Mina was an ambulance driver for the Navy hospital where Dr. Crandon was the physician in charge. They quickly renewed their acquaintance, and it wasn't long before they were a twosome. At first, her friends thought Dr. Crandon looked more like her father than a boyfriend, and later many a Beacon Hill hostess whispered that Dr. Crandon's new wife was "too attractive for her own good." "Let them talk, "Mina thought, "Dr. Crandon is a swell guy- the complete opposite of that no good John Rand." True, Dr. Crandon did have an eye for a pretty face and, young nurses were warned to avoid his advances. Nonetheless when Dr. Crandon whispered to Mina, he was on the verge of ending his second marriage, the attractive Mrs. Rand no longer sidestepped his long arms.

Dr. Crandon's charismatic charm swept the thirty- year-old ambulance driver off her feet faster than the downward current of Niagara Falls. As for Mr. Rand, he did not suspect his wife's affair. Initially, Earl Rand was stunned when his wife filed for divorce. However, he did not contest the action. When Mina Rand's divorce became final in September 1918, she quickly became the third Mrs. Le Roi Crandon.

End Notes

1. http://www.historynet.com/mina-crandon-harry-houdini-the-medium-and-the-magician.htm.
2. *Margery*, Thomas R. Tietze, Harper and Row Publisher, 1973, page 4.
3. Ibid., page 3.
4. http://www.debunker.com/texts/ruleofthumb.html.
5. http://www. Free Encyclopedia | Boston Brahmins.

Chapter 3
Boston, 1923

And this is good old Boston
The home of the bean and the cod
Where the Lodges speak only to the Cabots
And the Cabots speak only to God[1]

Dr. and Mrs. Crandon quickly moved into a four-story house at ten Lime Street on Beacon Hill. The elite neighborhood was the perfect address for Dr. Crandon as the Boston surgeon's family dated back to the Mayflower. Other Mayflower descendants included presidents John Adams, John Quincy Adams, Ulysses S. Grant, Franklin Delano Roosevelt, George H. W. Bush, and George W. Bush.

While the rest of the nation might be oblivious to what happened in the fall of 1620, in Boston the arrival of the Pilgrims on the Mayflower is still taken seriously. Cleveland Amory makes this point in his book, *The Proper Bostonian*, "When a Chicago banking firm of Lee Higginson & Co asked for a letter of recommendation, they replied 'His father was a Cabot and his mother a Lowell- in short the candidate could not be more acceptable.'" Unimpressed by the recommendation, the Chicago company replied "We are not contemplating Mr._____ for breeding purposes."[2]

In 1923 Boston had a caste system as rigid as any in India. Italians, such as Sacco and Vencetti, lived in East Boston; the Kennedys and other Irish Catholics lived in Dorchester. Jews streaming in from eastern Europe made Mattapan their home; while English descendants of the early Massachusetts settlers favored the suburbs particularly Wellesley. Those who remained in the hub lived in the tony Back Bay or exclusive Beacon Hill section of Boston.

As with so many proper Bostonians, the Crandons prized their four-story home. It was one of several elegant town houses that had been built and rebuilt for generations. The house, flanked by similar brick houses, faced a cobblestone alley. It was a fashionable district; once home to the Vanderbilt family and *Little Women* author Louisa May Alcott. Many of the homes on the neighboring Mount Vernon and Chestnut streets are now valued in the millions with those on near-by Beacon Street fetching at least five million dollars plus because of their view of the Boston Common.

Boston real estate is expensive as the city prides itself on being superior to the rest of the nation in breeding, academia, and taste in literature. The city was so refined that celebrated books, such as Walt Whitman's *Leaves of Grass* and Thomas Hardy's *Tess of the D'Urbervilles* were banned by the Watch and Ward Society. The prudish society even took offense to Keable's *Simon called Peter* because a man of the cloth engaged in premarital sex without shame. At the height of Watch and Ward Society's power in the late 19th and early 20th centuries, the Boston Public Library made sure that books that were deemed unfit for Boston readers were kept in a locked room.

Mina Crandon a paradox of sorts as well. While she was hardly a Puritan, she knew how to keep up appearances. For example, Mrs. Crandon would never refer to her husband as Le Roi. No it was always "Dr. Crandon wishes" or "Dr. Crandon prefers." Her husband who was used to the adulation of patients and nurses alike felt perfectly at home with this formality.

In 1923, however, standards were beginning to change all over the United States. With the advent of automobiles, parents became concerned about unchaperoned young people in cars on secluded country lanes. In Atlanta, Georgia, a grand jury went so far as to examine the link between the automobile and moral decline.

With so much big city sin, evangelists such as Billy Sunday and Aimee Semple McPherson were called into service. Sister Aimee began broadcasting from her Four Square Temple in Los Angeles in 1923. Over 5,000 people attended her evening service where the word of God was dramatized with special effects, such as thunder and lightning and music. By the end of 1923, Boston was beginning to roar like the rest of the country. The city's mayor, James Michael Curely, was serving a second term. He was hardly a model citizen. Curely was well-known for influence peddling, a charge which would later put him behind bars. Corruption was not only in City Hall but also in nearby Scully Square where burlesque acts played to packed crowds at the Old Howard. Boston also saw enthusiasm for professional sports. Boxing drew huge crowds at the Boston Garden, as did Red Sox games at Fenway Park.

The twenties with its free-wheeling attitude, short skirts, and bobbed hair seem made to order for the shapely Mina Crandon. Life at ten Lime Street was very pleasant indeed. Mina excelled as a homemaker and hostess. She quickly made the formal brick house a cozy home for Dr. Crandon and her ten-year old son, John. A cook, maid, and Japanese butler were at her disposal. Her merry laugh and twinkling blue eyes charmed everyone.

Few turned down an invitation to join Dr. and Mrs. Crandon for dinner. He was known to have a well-stocked wine cellar filled with champagnes, chardonnays, and aged burgundies to accompany lobster, roast duck, or prime rib. A typical meal might begin with a traditional Boston clam chowder made with heavy cream, salt pork, minced clams, and potatoes. During Christmas festivities, proper Bostonians favored prime rib, popovers, and scalloped potatoes, with Indian Pudding for dessert. In the summer, the entrée changed to grilled salmon accompanied by new potatoes and fresh peas, with fruit glace to clear the pallet Mina Crandon indulged in six-course dinners, charity four course-lunches, horseback riding in the Boston Common, while socialized with other doctor's wives, Kitty Brown and Mrs. Mark Richardson. Doctor Crandon preferred to focus on his surgery students at Harvard Medical School, a school few would link with psychic investigation. However, many of its professors, such as William James, have dabbled in the occult. James conducted a study on the medium, Lenore Piper, and championed mystical experiences in his book, *Varieties of Religious Experiences.* James even publicized his belief in mediumship in a 100-page paper given at the American Psychological Society.

Dr. Crandon, remained tight lipped about his interest in mediumship. As usual, he read late into the night. However, instead of his usual choice of literature- books about history and Abraham Lincoln, he chose a volume written by Professor W. J. Crawford, The *Reality of Psychic Phenomena* (1916). Dr. Crandon could not put it down. The book which documented a thorough investigation of the Kathleen Goligher Circle. Its author tried to explain psychic laws of direct voice and telekinetic activity in the séance room. Crawford, a lecturer in mechanical engineering at Queens University in Belfast took time to document the voices to measure and weigh ectoplasm, as well as to draw blueprints of psychic phenomena. As a result, he wrote three books on the subject: *The Reality of Psychic Phenomena* (1916*); Experiments in Psychic Science* (1919); and *The Psychic Structures in the Goligher Circle* (1921).

The last book was published posthumously because Dr. Crawford committed suicide on July 30, 1920. He had been in declining health and feared the onset of dementia. His last thoughts though were of psychic research and he left this note just before his death: "I have been struck down mentally. I was perfectly all right up to a few weeks ago. It is not the psychic work. I enjoyed it too well. I am thankful to say that the work will stand. It is too thoroughly done for any material loopholes to be left.[3]

What did the dedicated professor discover? First, he discovered that mediums such as Mrs. Z had the ability to do direct voice mediumship in which spirit speaks though an aluminum cone:

> Voices, not apparently the voice of the medium or of any of the sitters, speak from the air within or around the circle. They speak through thin metal cones or "trumpets" which seemingly float about in the air under psychic support, their function being to concentrate the voice sounds and thus make them more audible than they otherwise would be. Professor Crawford also meticulous weighed the medium before and after séances and discovered a lost ten pounds after the séances. Professor Crawford's research was verified by one of the spirits: "Mrs. Z., one of the voices, just before the break-up of the séance, gratuitously informed us that if we were to weigh the medium at the conclusion, we would find that she had lost 10 or more pounds, due to the phenomena occurring during the evening.[4]

When Dr. Crandon turned in for the night beside his sleeping wife, he thought, "Crawford certainly makes a good case for psychic phenomena. I will have to share his exploits with Margery in the morning."

End Notes

1. *The Proper Bostonians*, Cleveland Amory, E. P. Dutton, 1947, New York page 14.
2 .Ibid page 11.
3. http://www.survivalafterdeath.org/researchers/crawford.htm.
4. Ibid.

Chapter 4

It All Started as a Lark

You have the ability to become a very powerful medium.
Spiritualist minister

When Dr. Crandon mentioned Crawford's research on psychic phenomena, Mina thought the whole subject was "cockeyed." Spiritualism may have been at its height in 1923, but the spirited Mina preferred horseback riding on the Boston Common to parlor séances. Yes, she had had some experience with "spooks," and she had watched her brother Walter tip tables. But that was just kid stuff. Besides Walter was such a card she knew when he was kidding. Since Walter's death in 1911, Mina had had no contact with her dead brother and no reason to believe in spooks.

Hardly one to dwell on serious topics, Mina was more likely to be found flipping through the pages of *Vogue Magazine* than opening a leather-bound book from her husband's study. Unlike Dr. Crandon, she did not read late into the night on any subject especially books on psychic phenomena. In contrast to Dr. Crandon's scientific introduction to physical phenomena, his wife's psychic adventures began more or less as a lark. She decided to show Dr. Crandon how foolish he was, so she made an appointment with the minister of the First Spiritualist Church of Boston.

Before the meeting, Margery decided brisk ride through the Boston common her friend, Kitty Brown: She later told friends, "I knew perfectly well nothing would happen for it was all silly."[1] The pair didn't even bother to change before they visited the minster. "Let's take a chance," Mina told Kitty, "he probably won't even let us in the tea room in our riding clothes."

Much to their surprise, the Spiritualist did see the two young women. What happened next was to change the course of Mina's life. The minister turned out to be a medium who went into trance. "It wasn't long before two strange voices began to speak through the entranced medium. Each gave the name of Walter. One claimed that he was Mina's dead brother, Walter, and the other purported to be her dead uncle also named Walter."[2]

Mina was intrigued, but not convinced her brother was present, and asked for evidence. .She was flabbergasted when Walter replied," I hope you won't have the trouble with *those* riding boots that you had in Canada when you and I were riding. He then correctly named the ponies they had been riding that day."[3] Margery remembered the time her horse got mired in a swamp, and her wet riding boots became so tight, her brother had to cut them off with his pocket knife. It was a message only Walter could have given.

The spirit went to tell his sister that there was a more serious purpose to his visit. He explained that he was part of a group of spirits who wished to give proof of survival to the living. The group wanted to do more than give messages, they wished to provide scientific evidence with physical phenomena. "We are willing and eager to abilities with physical objects; we can do things that the living cannot do and which you cannot explain, and we like to prove this.[4] At the close of the session the medium turned to Mina and said, "You have the ability to become a very powerful medium."[5]

At the last statement, Mina burst into laughter. Becoming a medium was the last thing on her mind. "It is just too silly," she told Dr. Crandon. Intrigued, Dr. Crandon decided to pay a visit to the tea room medium a few days later. Careful not to reveal his identity, the doctor listened to the entranced medium give him a message from his deceased brother-in-law, Walter Stinson.

The next day, Dr. Crandon announced, "We shall have to have our own séance." Mina, who had no idea what a séance entailed, left the details to her husband. "The doctor knows best," thought Mina. Her instincts proved correct as Dr. Crandon plunged into the project. Not one to tackle any event without substantial research, Crandon looked up the details in Dr. W. J. Crawford's literature. Crawford advised table-tipping as a good beginning. It is a simple enough process in which a group sits round a table with their hands resting on it. According to Spiritualists, if spirit is present in the room, the sound of raps will be heard.

Often a code is established such as one knock means no, two knocks means yes. Later raps can indicate a letter of the alphabet. While some mediums prefer total darkness, red light is advised. In red light some illumination is provided but not enough to impede the production of ectoplasm needed to levitate the table. Another tip Crawford gave was to construct a table without nails to facilitate the process. Crandon told his carpenter build one exactly to Dr. Crawford's specifications.

The date for séance was set for May 27 1923. The venue was the fourth floor den in Crandon's home at ten Lime Street. The room was carefully chosen .Both Crandons agreed that the library was the best place for a séance. The eighteen-by-seventeen foot room with a nine-foot ceiling, was more than adequate. Besides, its location at the top of the house offered the most privacy. As a precaution against prying eyes, the servants were let go for the night, and Mina's son John was safely tucked in, so no one who disturb the séance.

On the night of the séance, the large sofa was pushed to the side of the fire place, and the séance table was positioned in the middle of the room. Six chairs were stationed around it. Dr. and Mrs. Crandon were joined by Mina's riding chum, Kitty Brown, and her husband Dr. Edison Brown, Frederick Adler, the superintendent in the building that housed Dr. Crandon's office, and another old friend, Alexander Cross. Cross, a frequent guest at ten Lime Street, had been brought up in Canterbury England, and he had spent many years in Shanghai as a customs officer. Since he was unable to find a suitable position in Boston, he made himself useful keeping records, running errands, and typing letters for Dr. Crandon.[6] When the heavyset affable Cross died in 1924 from a heart attack, both Dr. and Mrs. Crandon felt a keen loss.

However, on the evening of May 27th, Cross was just as curious as the rest of the old friends assembled in front of the séance table, half expecting the evening to end in failure, and other half hopeful that some slight movement might occur. As her chums sat poker-faced in the red light of the séance room in dead silence. Mina, who suddenly saw the humor in the whole situation, started saw the humor in the whole situation, started laughing at the strange sight. She stopped her fit of laughter only when her husband reminded her of the solemnity of the occasion. "Mina, this is a serious matter," intoned Dr. Crandon. [7]

Chastised, Mina calmed down and linked hands with her fellow sitters. They gently placed their finger tips on the round wooden table. "Suddenly there was a motion. Instantly all attention was on the wooded table before them. It slid laterally, very slightly but perceptively. Then it rose on two legs and fell to the ground with a crash"[8]

"Someone in the circle is a medium. Of that I am certain," said Dr. Crandon. To test his hypothesis, he asked each member of the group leave the room, one at a time. Kitty Brown left first then Dr. Brown, Adler, Cross and Dr. Crandon. The table continued to tip. Finally Mina rose and left the room. The table was immobile.[9] Dr. Crandon beamed with pleasure at his young wife. As for Mina, she thought the whole evening had been a lark!

End Notes

1. *A Life After Death*, S. Ralph Harlow, Schiffer Publishers, Atglen PA, 1983, pages 49- 50
2. Ibid., page 50
3. Ibid.
4. Ibid.
5. *Margery the Medium,* J. Malcolm Bird, Small, Maynard and Company, Boston 1925, page 16.
6. Ibid., pages 16-17.
7. Ibid., page 15
8. Margery, Thomas R. Tietze, Harper and Row, New York, NY, 1973, page 18.
9. Ibid.

Chapter 5

Table Tipping and All That Jazz

At times his (Walter's) voice would be close to my ear, whispering seem very personal comment about me or my family; at other times it would come from the corner of the room, or from outside the room, beyond the door piled waist high with books, or from the center of the table[1]

Professor S. Ralph Harlow

"Why such a fuss over a table moving?" thought Margery. "Well anything that makes Dr. Crandon happy, is fine with me." Though Margery was not enthralled with the idea of more séances, she was curious. "Maybe the spirits really are moving the table," she thought to herself.

As for Dr. Crandon, he thought of nothing else. A week later, he arranged for a second sitting. This time, he was more prepared and determined to make the sessions as scientific as possible. Mrs. Richardson was assigned the task of recording secretary. Once the table started tipping, Dr. Crandon established a code using raps rather than just tilting. The table tipped in what was agreed to be an affirmative way, and agencies ostensibly began to rap on the tabletop. In a short time the raps became stronger and a crude code was established.

Soon the table rapped out the names of several spirits, including those of Mark and John, the young sons of Dr. and Mrs. Richardson. The bereaved parents were thrilled by the communication from their deceased children. The spirit of Kitty Brown's mother also made her presence felt. However, one spirit came with great force. The most dominant personality was that of Margery's brother, Walter Stinson. In all, forty-four separate entities rapped out their messages on the table that year.[2]

On June 3, 1923, the table was especially animated. The spirit operator identified herself through a series of raps as Mrs. Caldwell, the mother of one of the sitters. Mrs. Richardson noted, "The table followed Caldwell out through the corridor, into the bedroom, rumpling all the mats in transit. Then, on request for more, the table started downstairs after him, when we stopped it to save the wall plaster."[3]

On July 23, Dr. Crandon decided to put the lights on so the phenomena could be viewed more clearly. He did so only after careful thought. Until that time the table tilting was done under red light frequently used by mediums who believe daylight is destructive to the production of ectoplasm, a gauze-like substance which is extruded from the orifices on the medium's body. If ectoplasmic rods were required, the table would remain still.

Apparently the table agreed with Dr. Crandon's decision. According to Mrs. Richardson's note, the table responded in a merry mood: "The table went around in quick joyous circles as though laughing with us-- then made a series of levitations, each higher than the one before-finally rising at least a foot and a half from the floor." The group timed the levitations-- one lasted sixteen seconds, another thirty.[4]

The table seemed to have a mind of its own. On September 21st, Mrs. Richardson noted, "Walter came in with the table and kept time with to the music by full levitation throughout the length of the session. He danced in the air with the table! The spirits did not stop at table-tilting. Soon psychic music was heard. One the most striking tunes according to Bird was "Taps" played "as on a bell so pure as to bear no vibration-- almost as if breathed out without the use of an instrument."[5]

Margery's table-tipping was not confined to the séance room. On October 18, she had an unsettling episode at a local restaurant. Margery took a seat at one of the smaller tables. "After her order was served, the lady opposite her called the waitress and asked her to put something under the table that is was making her seasick. It was in fact tilting sharply first to the right and then to the other. Margery withdrew in embarrassment, leaving her half-eaten meal.[6]

While table- tipping is a successful way to communicate with the other side, it is an awkward method. Words have to be laboriously tapped out- one rap for "A," two raps for "B," three raps for "C," and so on. "There must be a better method," Dr. Crandon thought. Having read the remarkable books on mediumship by William Jackson Crawford, Dr. Crandon knew of trance mediumship. In trance, a spirit could manipulate the vocal cords of an unconscious medium and speak directly.

"Trance is the next phase," Dr. Crandon announced to Margery with his usual air of authority. While the nurses in the hospital might accept his authority unconditionally, his wife had her reservations. "Sure," Margery thought, "I am going to go into trance just like that." Table-tipping might be a lark, but going into an unconscious state sounded risky. "Who knows if I will ever come back?" she thought to herself. Fearful of the unknown, Margery quickly rejected Dr. Crandon's request that she try trance: "I will do nothing of the sort- I don't want to miss any of the fun." However when her husband countered with, "Little sister will do exactly as big brother says." The table moved in approval.[7]

Psyche, Dr. Crandon's pet name for Margery, desired more than anything to please her husband. "How in the world will I enter trance. Guess I will have to try," she thought privately. Fortunately, trance control came naturally to the young blonde medium: "She signed deeply, closed her eyes, and swayed in the chair. Then in an abrupt voice there came through her lips the words 'I *said* I could put this through.'"[8] Walter had succeeded in coming through his entranced sister.

From then on, Margery's brother, Walter Stinson was the master of ceremonies. Obviously, his personality survived the train accident intact. He still had his wit and his famous whistle. When provoked he could swear as loudly as any sailor, especially after he had a few Boston side-car cocktails. His irreverent humor was present as well. When a group of clergymen attended a séance, Walter quipped, "Yes. Hell is completely up to date, we burn oi.l" [9]

Flushed with the initial success of table- tipping, trance, and séances, Dr. Crandon decided to construct a cabinet. According to researcher Hereward Carrington, a spirit cabinet was a "spiritual storage battery" where the psychic energy was concentrated enough to produce ectoplasm. A cabinet could be anything from a room portioned off by curtain to an actual piece of furniture.

While mediums, Ira and William Davenport, preferred a wood cabinet seven-feet high, six-feet wide and two-feet deep, Camp Silver Belle medium, Ethel Post Parrish, used a cabinet made of curtains that closed in the front. The cabinet that Dr. Crandon had constructed was somewhere in between the two versions. "It consisted of a three-part screen, six feet tall covered with a piece of black cloth that hung over the open front down to a level beneath Mina's head."[10] The purpose of the cabinet was to collect and contain ectoplasm which spirit extracted from the medium's body.

With her new spirit cabinet and her husband's constant encouragement, Margery's mediumship took off. By June 30, Margery had achieved such a depth of trance that Walter was able to speak through her and also relayed messages from other spirits. At first, Margery channeled he brother. His characteristic speech came through Margery's vocal cords. "Soon his the voice grew stronger, and later became independent of the medium's throat.

Soon Walter's voice could be heard from any part of the room, and was as clear and sharp as anyone in the room. Professor Ralph Harlow was fascinated by the independent voice of Walter as he wandered around the room, "At times his voice would be close to my ear, whispering seem very personal comment about me or my family; at other times it would come from the corner of the room, or from outside the room, beyond the door piled waist high with books, or from the center of the table."[11]

When asked how he managed to speak, Walter answered, "It is simple." He explained that he extracted a filmy substance called ectoplasm from Margery while she was in trance, and used the ectoplasm to build a voice box. He said the process was much like that of radio transmission which require an instrument: "while you use your own bodies to create voices, metal and paper and electricity in a radio, I use Margery's ectoplasm and my own vibrations" [12]

Under Walter's guidance, Margery's mediumship progressed rapidly. It wasn't long before she was able to do automatic writing. For example, while in trance under a red light, one spirit guide said, I'll draw something for you. Her hand then proceeded to draw a series of circles. Next, the message was printed by sprit in Latin, a language unfamiliar to Margery. *"Qui creavit te sine te non salvit te sine te."* The translation: "He who created you without any aid from you cannot save you without your help." [13]

On July 1, 1923, Dr William McDougall, Professor of Psychology, was invited to the group by one of the participants, Dr. Roback. Walter had a message for him as well: "We create our world for ourselves; we make our own heaven and hell." Walter then asked the professor to remember who had said this to him in the past-- as this person was the spirit communicator. [14]

Messages continued to come through in languages unknown to Margery- One came in Dutch " *Fred voer miteder*" translation: "Fred wants to take part." Messages came in other foreign languages including Chinese script that Aleck Cross, who had been stationed in China, was able to verify. The script received in automatic writing: "Kein Yuen hang li ching." Its English translation was: "The great General Kein Yuen is here." [15]

With such evidential messages, Cross joined other members of the ABC group in their enthusiastic belief in spirit communication. Unfortunately, Aleck Cross died within the year- too early to see Margery Crandon recognized as one of the world's great physical mediums.

End Notes

1. *Margery,* Thomas Tietze, Harper and Row, New York, 1943, page 21.
2. Ibid, page 20.
3. *Margery the Medium,* J. Malcolm Bird, Small, Maynard and Company, Boston, MA, page 35.
4. Ibid., pages 38-39.
5. ibid., page 61.
6. *Great Moments of Modern Mediumship,* Maxine Meiller, Saturday Night Press, England 2014, page 156
7. *Margery,* op.cite. pages 21-22.
8. *Margery the Medium*, J., opacity, page 48.
9. *The Truth About Margery*, Mark W. Richardson, 1947, page 92.
10. *Margery*, Thomas Tietze, op.cit, page 21.
11. *A Life After Death* , S. Ralph Harlow, Schiffer Publishers, Atglen PA, 1983, page 53.
12. Ibid., page 54.
13. *Margery the Medium*, op. cit, Boston, MA, page 50.
14. Ibid., page 50-51.
15. Ibid., page 52.

Chapter 6

Margery the Medium

The Crandons were not the kind of people whom it was easy to suspect of trickery. They allowed precautions to be taken. Investigators were encouraged to search the rooms in which the séances took place. [1]**Brian Inglis**

No other medium since Eusapia Palladino (1854-1918) had as much attention and controversy as Margery Crandon had. In fact, Margery exhibited many of the extraordinary powers of the Italian medium who tipped tables, levitated objects in the dark, produced apports, and communicated with the dead. Eusapia's spirit control was the deceased John King; while Margery's control was her deceased brother. Walter delighted in tipping and levitated tables, as well as producing spirit voices, and spirit writing.

With all this talent, it was inevitable that her fame would spread beyond the borders of Beacon Hill. Flushed with the success of these early experiment in the late spring and summer of 1923, Dr. Crandon wrote a letter detailing his wife's psychic abilities to Sir Arthur Conan Doyle (1879-1930), author of Sherlock Holmes mysteries and well-known Spiritualist.

Conan Doyle had also investigated Palladino's extraordinary mediumship. He was impressed by what he observed first-hand, table levitations, apports, and the materialization of spirits. All took in place in a dark séance room. Palladino was even able to produce impression of hands and faces of spirits in wet clay- a feat Margery Crandon would later duplicate.

However not everyone was as convinced as Sir Arthur. Other researchers such as Hereward Carrington were not so sure. Carrington knew that even genuine mediums such as Eusapia Palladino occasionally resorted to trickery. Female mediums were also known to use their sexual power over male investigators. Eusapia Palladino, for example, had a habit of climbing into the laps of the male investigators.[2] Rumors began to circulate that Palladino slept with some of the more attractive male sitters. Hereward Carrington, an ardent supporter, was believed to have had sexual relations with the peasant medium.[3]

Mediumship powers, if not properly used, have been known to weaken with time, which could explain differing opinions regarding Palladino's mediumship. Even the founders of Spiritualism did not escape this fate. The Spiritualist movement began on March 31, 1848, when two sisters Kate (1837-1892) and Maggie Fox (1833-1893) began to receive communications from the spirit of an itinerant peddler who made his presence known by loud raps in the basement of the Fox cottage. Soon twelve-year old and fifteen year-old girls established a code: one rap meant yes, two raps meant no, and three raps maybe. Then they progressed to a crude alphabet. One rap for A, two for B, three for C, and so forth. Slowly the peddler rapped out his story. Apparently the unlucky salesman had been murdered, and his body was buried underneath the Fox cottage. Many years later, Kate Fox made contact with the spirit of Benjamin Franklin. Sadly, both Maggie and Kate Fox eventually succumbed to alcoholism- diminishing their powers considerably.

Another medium, the Reverend Andrew Jackson Davis (1826-1910) fared better than the two sisters. Perhaps it was because of his illustrious guides: the spirit of the Roman physician, Galen, and the spirit of Swedish seer, Emanuel Swedenborg. Davis brought so many into the fold though books and lectures that the medical clairvoyant has come to be regarded as the John the Baptist of Spiritualism. He was so devoted to the cause that he became a medical doctor so he could legally practice his medical clairvoyance.

While modern Spiritualism began in the United States, it wasn't long before the movement crossed the Atlantic. As early as 1846, two years before the birth of Spiritualism, Queen Victoria was seeing the clairvoyant, Georgina Eagle, who appeared on stage billed as The Mysterious Lady.[4] Other English gentry who believed in the spirits included Sir Oliver Lodge (1851-1940) and Sir Arthur Conan Doyle (1858 - 1930). In his book, *The History of Spiritualism*, he praised Eusapia Palladino's mediumship.

Sir Arthur Conan Doyle carefully read Dr. Crandon's letter. "Could Mrs. Crandon be another Eusapia Palladino?" he wondered. For some unknown reason, -Doyle was not at all skeptical. In fact, he felt a flush of exhilaration, so much so that he could hardly wait to meet the American medium. Doyle, like many Spiritualists had been drawn to mediums because of personal loss. Both he and Lodge had lost sons in the Great War, only to find solace through mediums.

Lodge chronicled his communication with his deceased son, Raymond, through medium Lenore Piper in his book, *Life After Death*. Doyle would later detail the physical phenomena of Euspapia Palladino and Katie Cook's materialization in his two volumes of *The History of Spiritualism*. Even magician Harry Houdini, acknowledged Conan Doyle's contribution to Spiritualism: "Spiritualism has claimed among its followers numbers of brilliant minds – scientists, philosophers, professionals and authors those who allow themselves to be led by minds greater and more powerful than their own. Such a one is Sir Arthur Conan Doyle."[5]

When "Scientific America" wished to research mediums, they turned to Sir Arthur Conan Doyle for advice. Without hesitation he recommended Margery Crandon to James Malcolm Bird (1886-1964), the editor for "Scientific America." Bird trusted Conan Doyle implicitly. He had already sat with John C. Sloan, Gladys Osborne Leonard, William Hope, Ada Emma Deane, Evan Powell, and Maria Vollhardt on Sir Arthur Conan Doyle's recommendation.

In 1923 Bird gave an account of his research in *My Psychic Adventures*. The book, published by Scientific American, began with three questions fundamental to psychic research: "Do the phenomena upon which spiritism is based occur, any or all of them?" and "Under which conditions do these heretofore unexplained and unrecognized phenomena take place? " and "What makes these things happen?" [6]

Bird began his research in London with a séance with John Campbell Sloan (1879-1951), a Scottish direct voice medium: "The medium brought with him a long collapsible tin horn of two sections a a"trumpet." Mediums use a metal cone or trumpet as a megaphone through which a spirit can speak. In the trumpet séance, the trumpet "floats" about the darkened room so "spirit" voices can emanate through it. Sloan assembled twelve people to sit with him in complete and utter darkness. He then went into trance and the voice of his guide, White Feather, came through the trumpet. White Feather acted as a control, which is a medium in spirit who takes charge of the séance from the other side, thus ensuring orderly communication.[7]

According to Bird, "People flock to the room to communicate with the people, just as people flock to the room to communicate with spirits. Sometimes the control actually relays the messages, sometimes they appear to come direct from the communicating spirit." [8]White Feather, Sloan's control, was an American Indian who spoke in broken English, sometimes apologizing for his poor vocabulary. The séance began when White Feather entered what he called "the old box," the body of medium John Sloan. Soon voices were heard distinctly coming from the trumpet.

One voice was from an American spirit who announced his name as Cornelius Morgan. In an exchange of remarks, the Morgan's spirit who gave the researcher the evidence he sought. "Cornelius stated categorically and without hesitation or prompting, and addressing me unmistakably, that about three weeks previously on a Friday afternoon about 7:30, I had been walking across the Brooklyn Bridge with a lady and gentleman." When Bird's memory was sketchy, the spirit rebuked him for 'speech without thought-a "vicious' habit that was sure to get Bird in a peck of trouble".[9]

Bird was careful to note that the trumpet began to do a lot of traveling as the séance progressed. Bird reported, "On one occasion, it was heard inside the circle, outside, inside again, and once more outside in more rapid succession than I supposed to be possible by manual manipulation."[10] Bird also noted, "with the medium again apparently in the neighborhood of his seat, the trumpet traveled about the circle caressing each sitter somewhere about the face or head."[11]

In a second séance with John Sloan, spiritualist Ellis Powell came through to describe the spirit world: "No artist has ever painted, no poet has ever imagined the beauty of the land were in we dwell."[12] Bird also received a prophecy from the spirit that he would take a short journey over water to Leipzig. Malcolm Bird did indeed visit Leipzig, Germany enroute from Berlin to Munich. [13] While in Berlin, Bird was able to observe at close range the phenomena of apports. Physical mediums are known on occasion to bring small objects through the trumpet as gifts to the sitters. Malcolm Bird described his first apport séance with Frau

Vollhard who sat in the circle with a sitter on either side holding her hand in complete darkness:

> We had been so (seated) but a moment or two when the medium began to make her weird noises. These worked up to a climax quite rapidly. There was a faint rustling and the mediums groaned wildly and repeated and insisted that something happened. Dr. Schwab flashed his light and there on the table was a branch in the box- tree perfectly fresh. [14]

Excited by the positive evidence of spirit communication and apports in European séance rooms, Bird, an editor for *Scientific American Magazine* was eager to interview the American medium suggested by Sir Arthur Conan Doyle. Bird's first sitting with Margery Crandon was scheduled for November 15, 1923.

The séance was, unfortunately, marred by the presence of an "evil" spirit. As Bird could well verify there is only one thing more disturbing to a séance than the presence of a negative spirit. After some initial table tipping, Margery passed into trance and the spirit of Margery's irate brother, Walter, struck back at the evil spirit that was attempting to take over his sister's entranced body: "Suddenly with a particularly vicious snarl, the words 'Get the hell out of here' were articulated in the tones of mud-gutter rather than Back Bay"[15]

By November 26, Walter was in a better the mood for phenomena. For weeks the group had been discussing apports- particularly the possibility of bringing through a live apport. Walter was keen on the idea and began giving preparatory arrangements: "There must be a man in every room. We must do this scientifically. Do you trust these people?" [16]

The entire four-story house had to be searched to verify no live animal was present. The doors and windows closed 11:05 p.m. Present for the séance were Dr. and Mrs. Crandon, Dr. Brown , Aleck Cross, Mr. Adler, Dr. and Mrs. Mark Richardson, Charles Caldwell. When Dr. Brown led the way into the dining room, he saw something white on the floor that he picked up. It was, to every one's amazement, a live pigeon with a registration tag on one leg marked 1921 R I. The pigeon, transferred to Mrs. Brown's care, lived six to eight months.[17] Malcolm

Bird was most favorable impressed with Margery Crandon's November 1923 séances.

On December 1, 1923 Dr. and Mrs. Crandon sailed for Europe. Margery was giddy with excitement. She also had a case of nerves. Sometimes Dr. Crandon was cross if she did not give a good séance. However, Margery needn't have been concerned as she gave equally astounding séances. In Paris, "a make-shift cabinet was put up using a three-way screen with putting a shawl over the top, coming down about two feet in front. [18] Dr. Gustave Gelson and Professor Richet sat In the make-shift cabinet with the medium. Their efforts were rewarded by a levitation of the table in red light. The group applauded with "Bien, Bien," and added "Encore." The table obliged by levitating twice more to everyone's delight. [19]

Margery was equally triumphant when she gave a séance at her next port of call- London. On December 12, 1923, at eight p.m., she gave a sitting at the British College of Psychic Sciences. Mr. and Mrs. Hewatt McKenzie, heads of the college were present for the séance. Mr. Mc Kenzie sat at Margery's left and her husband sat at her right side. "Walter came through with tipping of the table and shortly after with a few words of greeting. There were raps on the floor, on one of the pillars, and on the center of the table. Walter whistled once inside the cabinet." [20]

Her séance at the college was quite evidential, Margery Crandon's strongest demonstration of mediumship occurred on December 16 at 5:00 p.m. during a séance for the British Society for Psychical Research held in Tavistock Square. Again a makeshift cabinet was assembled by curtaining off a corner of the room. The sitters were Mr. Eric Dingwall, the Society's research officer, his wife, another researcher, Mr. Fielding, and Lady Barrett, along with five other participants who linked hands. Dingwall held Margery's left hand, her husband held her right hand. Walter came through immediately. "'Good evening' on all sides of the table with the usual five tilts, He then levitated the table six separate times, from two to eight inches clear of the floor each time, in excellent red light." [21] Hewatt McKenzie and the rest of the group were suitably impressed.

Walter's exploits did not stop at the séance room door. He also managed to enter the photographer's studio. On December 12, Dr. and

Mrs. Crandon booked a session with Mrs. Ada Deane a well- known British spirit photographer. The year before on November 11, 1922, she and Estelle Mead sat for a two-minute Armistice silence at the Cenotaph in Whitehall, London. *A Daily Press* photographer took a picture of the platform. Their efforts were rewarded by a photograph of many spirit faces of veterans. The picture ran in the *Daily Press* the next day. When Margery sat for her spirit photograph with Ada Deane, Walter made his appearance as an "extra" about a foot above Margery's head, on her left.

Margery Crandon's final European session was given on December 17 1923, at the invitation of Sir Arthur Conan Doyle. After Dr. Crandon's vivid narrative of his wife's physical phenomena. Conan Doyle was most eager to observe Margery's mediumship first-hand. He was delighted to host a séance in his London flat that was just across from Victoria Station. What a séance it turned out to be! Margery sat in the make-shift cabinet made with a three-way screen covered by a rug hastily thrown hastily over the top. A ten-pound small square table was place in front of her: "With no light save that which filtered in accidentally from without, Walter came quickly, tilting the table in greeting. Then he did some very high levitation.[22] At times the table rose as high as eight inches. Walter's spirit gave his characteristic whistle. "Then he whistled in Sir Arthur's ear in recognition of his deafness; after which he whistled behind Lady Doyle. Next he shook the cabinet and brought the rug down over the psychic's head.[23] Walter was clearly having fun with the sitters.

By all accounts the séance was a great success. Walter not only came through his sister Margery with his usual whistle and clever patter, but he also was able to ring a bell without the aid of a human hand. When Conan Doyle left the séance room, he was convinced of the authenticity of Margery Crandon's mediumship. What is more, he was intrigued by the thirty-five- year-old blonde medium. Why not? Margery, who never charged for her services, was as generous as she was beautiful.

1923 turned out to be a banner year for Margery Crandon. The young medium amazed sitters from Boston to France and England. J. Malcolm Bird urged her to go public, suggesting she take the name "Margery." In 1925 J. he wrote her biography entitled *Margery the Medium*. Mrs. Le Roi Crandon of Beacon Hill smiled as she read the first pages of *Margery the Medium*. Who would ever guess that she was a medium?

End Notes

1. http://www.michaelprescott.freeservers.com
2. *Ghost Hunters: William James and the Search for Scientific Proof of Life After Death*, Deborah Blum, New York, Penguin Press, 2006.
3. *The Spiritualists*, Ruth Brandon, New York, Alfred E. Knopf, 1983.
4. http://www.emmalouiserhodes.com/articles/concise-history-of-spirtualism.php
5. Ibid. http://www.emmalouiserhodes.com/articles/concise-history-of-spirtualism.php
6. *My Psychic Adventures*, J. Malcolm Bird, Scientific America, 1923, page 5.
7. Ibid., page 55.
8. Ibid., page 57.
9. Ibid., pages 66-67.
10. Ibid., page 78.
11. Ibid. page 78. Ibid.
12. Ibid., page 88.
13. Ibid., pages 90-91.
14. Ibid., pages 232-233.
15. *Margery the Medium*, J. Malcolm Bird, Small, Maynard and Company, Boston, page 118.
16. Ibid., page 129.
17. Ibid., pages 127-131.
18. Ibid., page 135.
19. Ibid., pages 135-6.
20. Ibid., page 136.
21. Ibid., page 138.
22. Ibid., page, 139.
23. Ibid. page 152.

Chapter 7

Phenomena and More Phenomena

The sitters witnessed phosphorescent lights and movements of objects at a distance from the medium, as well as feeling touches from invisible hands while both Crandon and 'Margery' were under their control.
Hereward Carrington[1]

Nineteen twenty four promised to be a good year for Margery. In fact it looked like it was going to be a good year for women everywhere. They were advancing in society since they had received the right to vote in 1920. They quickly adopted a new look to match their emancipated spirit. Ladies tossed out the old-fashioned corsets the Gibson favored. They preferred the short skirts and straight lines of the chemise. Some young girls even wrapped cloth around their chests to achieve the flattering silhouette that was all the rage. Bobbed hair became the most radical change of all. These young women became known as "flappers," a term which came from a tendency of young women in the early 1920s to leave their galoshes unfastened so they flapped as they walked. While Dr. Sigmund Freud viewed the flappers' androgynous style as a "gigantic mistake." Author, F. Scott Fitzgerald loved their exuberance: "They are just girls, all sorts of girls, their one common trait being that they are young things with a tremendous talent for living."[2]

When thirty-six year old Margery Crandon bobbed her hair and shortened her skirts in 1924, she looked ten years younger. The new look suited her blonde locks and slim figure. Never before had Margery felt so attractive. All eyes were on her that year, not only for her flair for fashion, but also for her talent as a medium.

Mediumship, though still a novelty for Margery, was not a new phenomenon. Attempts to communicate with the dead date back to the *Old Testament* when King Saul visited the Witch of Endor to seek advice from the spirit of the prophet Samuel on an upcoming battle. While Dr. Crandon's Puritans shunned witches, mediumship became fashionable in the United States with the rise of Spiritualism movement. It had begun in 1848 with the Fox sisters, and soon spread like a July wild fire across the United States. Trance mediums such as the Davenport Brothers and Paschal Beverly Randolph were also popular on stage in the mid-1800s. Later, D. D. Home amazed audiences in America and abroad by demonstrating levitation before the astonished eyes of royalty and commoners alike.

Hereward Carrington listed Daniel Douglas Home (1833-1886) and William Stainton Moses (1839-1892) as noted physical mediums in his volume called *The Story of Psychic Science.* Each had his own unique gift. William Stainton Moses, an Oxford graduate and clergyman, was known for his automatic writing, raps, lights and scents in the séance room. Moses also had the remarkable gift of slate-writing. His method was simple. He bound two clear slates together with a piece of chalk in the middle and placed it on a table in the séance circle. When the slates were later opened, they were filled with messages written directly by spirit entities. Carrington felt the direct spirit writing was genuine: "Difficult as it may be to believe in their realty, it is equally difficult to believe that Moses resorted to petty tricks in order to deceive his personal friends for a number of years." [3]

Hereward Carrington formed an even more favorable impression of D. D. Home. He credited with "movement of objects without contact, raps, levitations of tables and other objects, levitation of his own body and elongation of his body, lights, materializations, playing upon physical instruments, ect., were all observed at his séances." [4] Furthermore, researchers such as Dr. William Crookes were able to observe the phenomena in daylight since Home rarely did his séances in the dark.

Physical mediumship such as that exhibited by Home and Moses had its heyday in the Victorian era. By the 1920s physical mediumship was on the decline in Spiritualist churches. It was replaced by trance mediumship, which later became known as channeling. Just as science was developing instruments sophisticated enough to photograph, record and verify phenomena, fewer and fewer physical mediums were available for laboratory studies.

Margery Crandon was the last of these great physical mediums. When she returned from abroad in late 1923, Margery was determined to develop her gifts of materialization and independent writing. She resumed séances at ten Lime Street on December 30, 1923- this time with a few toys. Spirits love to play with bells, tambourines, and gongs, as well as move small objects such as flowers. Three roses and a Chinese gong with a stick to strike it were placed on a small table in the séance room. In the darkness of the séance circle, two of the roses were deposited in the Dr. Caldwell's right hand, and "at another moment the gong was struck with the stick several times in time and in tune with the Victrola."[5]

On Valentine's Day, 1924, Walter had some fun with the ladies. Mrs. Lit Zelman said to Walter, "I have three red, red, red, roses for you. The playful spirit replied, "I have you a yaller, yaller , yaller rose, and Kitty (Mrs. Brown) I have brought you a yaller, yaller, yaller rose, and Ma I have brought you a yaller, yaller, yaller rose." [6] Then, according Malcolm Bird who was present in the séance room, he witnessed single roses that landed in the laps of he three ladies addressed. When the lights were turned on each had in her lap, "a small rosebud, yellow and crumpled with stems obviously fresh cut." [7]

During the month of March, Malcom Bird observed spirit flowers, curtain rings, and an illuminated ashtray placed on the table by unseen hands during a séance. Soon flowers caressed the faces of sitters, and landed in their laps as they sat in the darkened circle. On March 17th, a carnation hit Margery on the head. Another sitter, Laura C., felt a curtain ring sail over her head. An illuminated ashtray was seem to move around the circle. By the end of March, Walter had had his fill of séance toys. "On the thirtieth with these and other small objects rather cluttering up the table, Walter picked them all up, one after another, and threw them about the room."[8] Sitters experienced not only flying objects and flowers, but also touches of spirit fingers and hands. At times they felt caresses on their legs and feet and sometimes on their arms. Margery described the sensations as "soft pinches of the fingers," while Mrs. Richardson described the sensations "as though some soft object like a rubber ball or animal's paw had been gently stroked or pressed against my calf and ankle."[9] Sitters at Margery's séance were especially delighted to receive apports. Many received flowers and jewelry. Dr. Richardson's young daughter was delighted to have a nice opal placed in her palm my spirit. Where it came from is anyone's guess. Walter just joked I've been robbing graves." [10]

Other phenomena occurred as well. All spring strong cool breezes were felt in the séance room. According to Malcolm Bird's records, there were drops in temperature as much as twenty degrees. He noted on May 4, 1924, the temperature in the séance room plummeted from sixty-eight degrees to forty-two degrees. How did Walter do it? He explained, "For the work tonight I will have to use the kid (Margery) only, because I find your brains in such poor condition. When I use your brains there are cold breezes and a drop in temperature. When I have the kid alone, none of these effects is produced."[11] Apparently Walter took his energy from the "brains" of the sitters, which when lacking vitality caused the temperature to go down.

Strange lights were also observed during 1924 séances. Frequently, sitters in Margery's circle noticed a red light around the Victrola. Sometimes the Victrola would stall during the séances, so it was brought to Comstock's shop where engineers and his electricians examined it and gave the Victrola a "blanket guarantee." That supposedly put an end to the phenomena. However, "that night, during the séance, it stalled six times, slowed three times, and got so hot, one could hardly truck it," [12] observed Malcolm Bird. He also noted a red light around the Victrola. When the Victrola stopped, the red light also disappeared. Observers also saw lights in the circle after the initial red light was extinguished. For example, séance records from June 22 record: "Just after the red light was put out at the beginning of the sitting, a phosphorescent light was seen on the medium's chest." Kitty Brown and Dr. Comstock also saw the light which remained on Margery's chest for about four minutes before it returned to its original position.[13]

With so much phenomena present, the two investigators Malcolm Bird and Hereward Carrington wanted to validate the psychic events scientifically. Observation was one thing, but science prefers hard physical evidence over the mind, which can be easily deceived. They were not the first investigators to face this dilemma. Dr. Geley Geley of the Institute Metapsychique International devised his own method to test Polish medium, Franek Kluski. The researcher attended fourteen séances with Kluski in Paris between November and 8th and December 31, 1920 . According to Geley, "A bowl of hot paraffin was placed in the room and according to Kluski spirits dipped their limbs into the paraffin and then into a bath of water to materialize."[14] If a spirit hand was thrust into the melted wax several times, an impression would be left in the form of a paraffin glove.

Malcolm Bird carefully studied over twenty of these paraffin gloves at Geley's small museum at the Institute and was astounded at the detail: "The anatomical detail which they show is altogether amazing, and one can accept the statement of artist and sculptures that they are unquestionably made from a living model."[15] Furthermore Dr. Geley always added coloring or chemicals at the last moment to insure the paraffin wax was not switched. He was convinced that the paraffin gloves stood up to further analysis with the added color or chemical paraffin." [16] Lydia, the Crandon's Swedish maid did as requested and brought the bucket of hot paraffin upstairs for the séance. Bird then placed the paraffin bucket as requested by Walter on Margery's left, and next to it, a bucket of cold water. Walter fussed a bit, asking the paraffin bucket to be placed in front of the entranced medium and then dismissed the bucket of cold water stating: "I don't need it, I make my own cold." [17]

With characteristic good humor, Walter called out, "Now me for a Turkish bath." According to Bird the swishing sounds were heard in the dark séance room. After a few more jibes Walter ended the session. "Now Birdie, I will give you a sensation, when you carry that pail, I am in it."[18] Birdie did as he was instructed: "At last he permitted me to go over to the corner near where I had placed the pail and get the hand. He instructed me carefully as to just where I could find the 'baby' wrapped in black cloth. [19] The paraffin hand created was in perfect details with nails, lines, and wrist markings. Bird included photographs of the hand impression made on May 17 along with later spirit impressions in his book, Margery the Medium. From a scientific standpoint, the physical evidence was impressive

Even more startling phenomena of the summer occurred on June 24, 1924. The medium's cabinet was literally dismembered with Malcolm Bird inside. He reported that Walter came through his entranced sister and asked Bird to join Margery in the cabinet. Bird obliged by sitting on the floor inside the cabinet. According to Bird, the cabinet had had quite a lot of activity that evening from slight sound and vibrations to screws and thumbtacks falling from time to time from the cabinet: "After a number of noises indicating falling screws or thumbtacks, there fell down upon Bird and Margery what was assumed to be the top clothe of the cabinet, and they had some difficulty extricating themselves from under it."[20] Fortunately, Dr. Hereward Carrington was one of the sitters. He corroborated Bird's detailed report of the incident to "Scientific American."

On another occasion, the group experimented with wooden blocks. Walter tried to spell out messages by manipulating the blocks in total darkness. Everyone heard the thumps of four blocks that were deposited at Harlow's feet. Walter had brought through a message from Harlow's deceased sister, Anna. When the light were turned on, much to Harlow's delight, there on the floor near his chair were "four blocks perfectly aligned, spelling "Anna."[19] Walter then relayed messages regarding her husband and four children.[21]

Perhaps the most astonishing phenomena was the ectoplasmic hand that Walter produced on several occasions. When researcher, S. Ralph Harlow, placed a handkerchief on the table and requested that Walter manipulate the hand to pick it up, the hand picked up the handkerchief, and waved it. Next, Dr. Brewer Eddy asked Walter to take a twenty-five cent piece from his hand and place in someone else's hand. The Reverend S. Ralph Harlow had the pleasure of receiving the coin: "Immediately the tiny ectoplasmic fingers lifted the coin from Dr. Eddy's hand, and Walter's voice said, Parson, hold out your palm. I did so, and the quarter dropped into my fingers."[22]

End Notes

1. http://michaelprescott.freeservers.com/the-two-faces-of-margery.html.
2. http://www.anzasa.arts.usyd.edu.au/ahas/flappers_overview.
3. *Story of Psychic Sciences,* Hereward Carrington, Kessinger Publishing; Facsimile Ed edition, March 1997, page 194.
4. Ibid., pages 194-195
5. *Margery the Medium*, J. Malcolm Bird., Small, Maynard and Company, Boston, page 164.
6. Ibid, page 165.
7. Ibid., page 169.
8. Ibid., page 166
9. Ibid., page 178.
10. *Fate Magazine,* Marion Nestor, "The Margery Mediumship- I Was There," Fate Magazine, April 1985, page 84
11. *Margery the Medium*, op. cit., page 190.
12. *Margery the Medium*, op. cit., page 329.
13. *Margery the Medium*, op. cit., page 366.
14. http://en.wikipedia.org/wiki/Franek_Kluski
15. *Margery the Medium*, op. cit. page 333.
16. Ibid., page 338.
17. Ibid., page 339
18. Ibid., page 339.
19. Ibid., page 314.
20. *A Life After Death*, S. Ralph Harlow, Schiffer Publishers, Atglen PA, 1983, page 59.
21. Ibid., 59.
22. Ibid., page 56.

Chapter 8

Scientific American Committee

*Both read the Bible day and night
But thou read'st black where I read white* .**William Blake**

As Malcolm Bird sealed the flap of the envelope with his report to *Scientific American,* he was confident of his research. The associate editor knew the value of meticulous research and had checked his facts carefully. He had insisted scientific records be kept of temperature changes, lights and breezes, along with verbatim transcription of Walter's comments. He had been especially diligent when he oversaw the paraffin gloves because he knew for the materialistic men of science, physical evidence was most important. While shaken up by the recent cabinet episode, Bird was also delighted. His report would described the recent dismantling in detail. "Thank God, Carrington was there to testify as well."

Bird heaved a sigh of relief at his last thought. *Scientific American* was a stickler for accuracy. Founded in 1845 by Rufus M. Porter, the publication grew from a single page newsletter describing new inventions to a prestigious monthly magazine in 1921. Its readers eagerly looked forward to the latest in scientific research accompanied by wood-cut illustrations. *Scientific American* was known for its carefully edited articles back by scholarly research.

Malcolm Bird's report was well received. On July 23, 1924 *Scientific America* accepted Margery Crandon as a candidate for the $2,500 prize offered by the magazine to the first person to produce a genuine psychic photograph and other physical psychic manifestations, under scientific controls, to the satisfaction of their committee. On the Scientific American Committee were some of the most noted names in parapsychology and science-Harvard Professor William McDougall, M.I.T. physicist Dr. Daniel F. Comstock, Dr. Walter Franklin Prince, and psychic researcher Hereward Carrington. Later, magician Harry Houdini requested to be included on the committee.

45

The Medium Who Baffled Houdini

The prize money was soon doubled to $5,000, a substantial sum in 1924. Margery was excited about the event, not because of the prize money, which she already said would be declined. Instead she was excited by the prospect of showing up learned men of science who so often scoffed at psychic activity. "It is high time they pay attention," she thought. "Plus Dr. Crandon and Walter think I am a shoo in!"

Cheered on by the spirit of her dead brother and her learned husband, Margery just "knew" she would pass any test the men of science devised. Hadn't she already made the bell box ring and produced spooky fingerprints? "The last test Birdie came out with was the toughest," she thought. She cringed at the idea of making paraffin replicas of spirit hand. It turned out fine with a little help from Birdie and Walter. "What more was there?" she thought. Whatever test the professors from Harvard and M.I.T. came up, with Margery was confident, she would pass with ease. After all, hadn't she encouraged her twelve year-old son to keep his chin up? Now it she was ready to follow the same advice she had dispensed to John "As long as you try everything will work out."

"Of course, the kid wasn't too keen on the spooks," Margery sighed. Perhaps she should have protested more when Dr. Crandon locked John in his room during the séances. "It might scare the kid," she said when he insisted on strict controls giving the servants the night off and locking John's door. A good boy, John didn't complain but still his mother worried. "We probably should send him to prep school as Dr. Crandon suggested. After all, he knows best." Margery almost always acquiesced to the demands of her older and wiser husband.

Still, things had been going smoothly at ten Lime Street. Every evening saw séances, guests, and now *Scientific American* investigations. "It will be the cat's pajamas to see the faces on the committee members when Walter starts moving the trumpet around," she thought. "Besides, both Dr. Crandon and Malcolm Bird say I owe it to science. We'll see," smiled Margery, picturing the stunned faces on the men of the Scientific America Committee when Walter made his entrance.

By July 1924, the Committee consisted of four members: Dr. William McDougall, of Harvard University; and a former president of the American Society of Psychical Research, Dr. Daniel F. Comstock, Massachusetts Institute of Technology professor; Dr. Walter Franklin

Prince, President of the Society for Psychical Research; and Hereward Carrington, distinguished British researcher and Scientific American editor. Malcolm Bird agreed who to act as secretary for the Committee, and Dr. Austin C. Lescaboura, another editor on the *Scientific American,* would assist in arranging the tests since he had been involved in previous investigations at ten Lime Street.

Professor William McDougall (1871-1938) was the most skeptical. Born in Lancashire, England, he had been a professor of psychology at Oxford University before joining the staff at Harvard. In 1920 when he became president of the Society for Psychical Research, He joined a long line of prestigious presidents who included Henry Sidgwick, William James, Sir William Crookes, F. W. Myers, Sir Oliver Lodge, Charles Richet, Eleanor Sidgwick, and Andrew Lang.

Professor McDougall was not the first psychologist to analyze a medium. Professor William James had observed medium, Lenore Piper. He believed that she was able to contact the dead, although he was not sure if she used telepathy or mediumship. He also felt that psychic phenomena was legitimate and deserved its place in science: "If you wish to upset the law that all crows are black, it is enough if you prove that one crow is white. My white crow is Mrs. Piper."[1]

McDougall was equally intrigued by psychic phenomena, but careful not to commit himself--even though he had observed five months of Margery Crandon's séances at close range at ten Lime Street. He knew that the Society for Psychical Research had been fooled many times. When Richard Hodgson investigated Helena Petrovna Blavatsky, co-founder of the Theosophical Society, he caught her in trickery. In 1905, Hodgson did find Lenore Piper more credible than Blavatsky. Both he and William James found Piper's trance communications genuine. Even though her control, the French physician, Dr. Phinuit, did not speak French while Mrs. Piper was in trance, the messages given were evidential.

Eusapia Palladino, on the other hand, along with mediums Kate Fox and Henry Slade were found wanting by the Society. With its leaders under suspicion, Spiritualists objected to the atmosphere of extreme mistrust and even accused the Society of fraud. Noted scientists such as Gustav Geley also leveled criticism at the Society for Psychical

Research. He was particularly incensed by the society's report on the medium, Eva C. Sir Oliver Lodge summed up this sentiment in his book, *The Survival of Man,* published in 1909: "It has been called a society for the suppression of facts, for the wholesale imputation of imposture, for the discouragement of the sensitive, and for the repudiation of every revelation of the kind which was said to be pressing itself upon humanity from the regions of light and knowledge."[2]

Against this criticism of overly skeptical attitudes, the Society strove to maintain high scientific standards of investigation. As a past-president of the American Society for Psychical Research, Dr. McDougall would need more than a trumpet flying around the room, a wealthy host, or a beautiful medium to convince the group of authentic paranormal events.

The current president of the American Society for Psychical research, Walter Franklin Prince (1863-1934) was more empathetic. An Episcopal minister who was interested in abnormal psychology and parapsychology, Prince was as fascinated with Margery Crandon as he had been with Pearl Curran. The St. Louis, Missouri medium channeled a spirit guide, Patience Worth, a spirit who claimed to have lived in Dorsetshire, England in the seventeenth century and to have been killed in America. Using the Ouija board, automatic writing and direct voice, Patience Worth dictated through Mrs. Curran in a late medieval English prose and poetry. The result was a mass of poems, six novels, and a prize-winning play. Prince praised the study of Patience Worth stating: "It must be regarded as the outstanding phenomenon of the age." Prince continued to remain a life-long friend to Margery Crandon.

While Dr. Prince, who had attended Yale University and Drew Divinity School, and was trained in spirituality, M.I.T. physicist Dr. Daniel F. Comstock specialized in material science. He became famous as one of the inventors of the Technicolor process of motion pictures in color. Professor Daniel Comstock also made the news when he championed William James Sidis (1898 -1944) an American child prodigy with an IQ estimated to be 250-300. Comstock had already predicted that the boy would someday be the greatest mathematician of the century. Sadly, Sidis who had entered Harvard at age eleven suffered a break down in his twenties and from then on avoided the field of mathematics. More successful as physicist than a seer, Dr. Comstock founded Comstock and Westcott and continued to devote his time to research in the fields of Technicolor and parapsychology.

Of the four researchers, Hereward Carrington, the author of several books on psychic research, had the most experience. His books included *The Physical Phenomena of Spiritualism*, 1907; *Eusapia Paladino and Her Phenomena*, 1909; *The Problems of Psychical Research*, 1914; *Modern Psychical Phenomena*, 1919; and *Your Psychic Powers and How to Develop Them*, 1920. Although his books would eventually number over 100, the prodigious author had originally been more interested in becoming a stage magician than exploring the psychic world. His interest in the paranormal was piqued when he read well-documented cases recorded by Fredric W. H. Myers and other serious psychical researchers. By 1924, Carrington had become well known in England and the United States.

Wherever he went on both sides of the Atlantic, Carrington's reputation as a tough investigator preceded him. The distinguished British researcher had been chosen by the British Society of Psychical research to study the medium, Eusapia Palladino. In his book about her, he advanced the idea that Spiritualistic theory was the most reasonable hypothesis for explaining her physical phenomena. Later, after Palladino was caught cheating in a New York séance, he would have to reconsider this view.

Carrington was also familiar with the work of Kathleen Golighter, the medium investigated by Dr. William Crawford. Carrington noted that "one of the first things which Dr. Crawford did was to place the medium on a scale, and note her exact weight. The stool or table to be levitated was also weighed. Now during the levitation that followed, he found by repeated trials that the weight of the medium increased by the weight of the table: for example, if the table weighed four pounds, the medium weighed four pounds more approximately during the levitation."[3]

Margery did not need to fear the forty-four-year-old Carrington, as the psychic investigator was smitten with her. He remained convinced of the validity of her mediumship at the end of the investigation. In fact, his support of her mediumship was so staunch that he broke with the American Society for Psychical Research over a disagreement concerning her mediumship. He later formed his American Psychical Institute in 1933.

The Medium Who Baffled Houdini

When Harry Houdini heard that the Scientific American Committee was leaning favorably toward Margery Crandon's mediumship, he was determined to be on the panel. After Houdini's wishes were made known, Malcolm Bird sent this letter that received a positive reply:

Scientific American,
233 Broadway, New York.
June 18, 1924.

Mr. Harry Houdini,
278 West 113th St.,
New York City.

My Dear Mr. Houdini:
    As you will observe when you get your July "Scientific American," we are engaged in the investigation of another case of mediumship. Our original idea was not to bother you with it unless, and until, it got to a stage where there seemed serious prospects that it was either genuine, or a type of fraud which our other Committeemen could not deal with. Regardless of whether it turns out good or bad, there will be several extremely interesting stories in it for the "Scientific American" and these will run in the August and following issues. Mr. Munn feels that the case has taken a turn which makes it desirable for us to discuss it with you. Won't you run in, at your convenience, to take lunch with one or both of us, and have a talk with Mr. Munn? Better call me in advance, and make sure that he and I will be in at the time you select.

Faithfully yours,
 J. Malcolm Bird,
Associate Editor.

    After Bird issued the invitation, it was only a matter of a few days before Harry Houdini became the fifth member of the Scientific American Committee.

End Notes

1. Gardner Murphy, Robert O. Ballou. (1960). *William James on Psychical Research*. Viking Press. p. 41.
2. *The Survival of Man*, Sir Oliver Lodge, Moffet Publisher, New York, NY 1908.
3. *The Story of Psychic Sciences*, Hereward Carrington, Kessington Publishers, Facsimile Edition, March 1997, pages 195-196
4. http://www.pbs.org/wgbh/amex/houdini/sfeature/margery1.html

Chapter 9

Enter Harry Houdini

If you give this award to a medium without the strictest examination every fraudulent medium in the world will take advantage of it. **Harry Houdini**[1]

The great Harry Houdini had a humble start in life. He was born Ehrich Weisz on March 24, 1874, in Budapest, Hungary. He was the fourth son of Mayer Samuel Weisz, a religious teacher, and his second wife, Cecilia Steiner. When Ehrich was two, his family immigrated to Appleton, Wisconsin where his father took a job as Rabbi Weiss. However, by the time Ehrich was eight, his father, considered old-fashioned by the congregation, and was replaced by a younger rabbi. Soon his son was selling newspapers and shining shoes to help the impoverished family.

At twelve, Ehrich was smitten by magic after his father took him to see a magic show. Soon the ambitious lad hopped a freight train to Kansas City to seek his fortune. He was taken in by an older couple and eventually was reunited with his family who had relocated to New York City.

While living in the slums of New York, Ehrich worked hard as a messenger, necktie cutter, and photographer's assistant. Ehrich's true love remained magic. He read everything he could find on the great magicians. He was particularly fascinated by the French magician, Jean Eugène Robert-Houdin (December 6, 1805 – June 13, 1871). Robert-Houdin had amazed audiences by suspending his son in midair. He also used the boy as an assistant in the 'Second Sigh" trick, in which the blind-folded young man correctly identified all the items held up by members of the audience. In another trick, the magician "allowed an Arab to shoot at him with a marked bullet, but instead of killing him, the bullet was found between his teeth."[2]

Ehrich Weiss idolized Robert-Houdin so much so that when became a professional magician he changed his first name to Harry and added an "i" to Houdin to become Harry Houdini. Initially, he had little success in magic and had to rely on card tricks by billing himself as the King of Cards in sideshows. Undaunted, Houdini teamed up with his brother, Dash, to focus on escape acts as the Houdini Brothers. In 1893, while performing with Dash at Coney Island, " he met and married another performer, Wilhelmina Beatrice (Bess) Rahner. His wife replaced Dash in the act now known as the Houdinis.

In 1895, the Houdinis joined the Welsh Brothers Circus Harry did magic, where they performed a trick called "Metamorphosis." They amazed audiences by switching places in a locked trunk. However, during slow periods the couple had to work as traveling clairvoyants. Sometimes, Harry would don a turban and pretend to be a Swami; on other occasions, Bess would pretend to be a trance medium on stage. If the questions to the "medium" became too specific for Bess to answer, she would conveniently swoon.

Harry did not have to make a living as a fake medium for long. Once he mastered the art of publicity, and became the King of Handcuffs descended on Europe boasting there was no set of handcuffs that could not be opened by the Great Houdini. Within months, he was performing to sold-out audience. Even though he was making large fees as an escape artist, and no longer impersonated mediums, he still remained interested in the supernatural. After the death of his seventy-two year- old mother, Cecilia Weiss, in July of 1914, he became even more intrigued by the idea of communicating with the dead. Houdini was genuinely grief-stricken: "He immediately canceled his engagement even though in Denmark breach of contract was a criminal offense. Herr Beretow took sympathy on his grieving star and Houdini repaid him by taking out a large-boxed ad in the circus's program thanking him for his display of sensitivity."[3] He managed to leave Germany just as World War I was brewing.

With the war raging in Europe, Houdini put his magic career on hold and donated time to the war effort. He enjoyed entertaining the troops with his "Money for Nothing" in which he pulled gold coins out of the air. Each coin was then given a soldier heading overseas. Houdini personally gave away $7,000 (the equivalent of $250,000 in today's currency). He also gave additional money for a hospital ward which he dedicated to his mother."[4]

For all his bravado, Houdini had a sentimental streak along with his generous nature. For instance, he never failed to miss an opportunity to refer to his mother and his wife his two sweethearts. He was to remain for the most part a "straight arrow" all his life. His only indiscretion seems to be with Charmian- London- the beautiful widow of author Jack London. In the fall of 1917 when she London was in New York, she wrote to her friend Harry to inform him that she was planning to relocate to New York: "Someday, at exactly the right time, I shall tell you more about this past year, and the other remarkable experience I have had that I've really carved out for myself. This is your letter. Please destroy it (but don't forget it) C.L" [5] If Houdini did have an affair with her, it was brief because she returned to California in the spring of 1918. Houdini also experienced other changes. "I am drifting away from vaudeville and with the exception of my European dates have no plans to return," he wrote to his friend Quincy Kilby. [6]

It was not Charmian London, who lured Houdini to California; it was the film industry. However, the permissive atmosphere of Hollywood was at odds with morality of the rabbi's son: "With temptation all around him in Hollywood, and Charmian London on her ranch only forty miles north, Houdini decided to make a very public show of affection toward Bess. The ploy worked wonders. On the twenty-fifth anniversary of their wedding, June 22, 1919, Bess was overcome with emotion when the band played the Wedding March.[6] The public display of affection was proof of the childless couple's abiding love for each other. Sure, their marriage was rocky at times; partly due to the demands of Houdini's career, and partly due to Bess's alcoholism. However, the couple never seemed closer.

After all, the couple who lived on separate floors of their New York brownstone always kept their differences private. In public they presented a united front as they maintained a grand life together entertaining the crème de la crème of society. In England, the Houdinis forged a strong friendship with Sir Arthur Conan Doyle, the famous author and creator of Sherlock Holmes. Houdini found Conan Doyle most affable and "as nice and sweet as any mortal I have ever met." Doyle found the great magician "as far and away the most curious and intriguing character I have ever encountered." [7]

Both men were interested in mediumship, but from different angles. When Houdini showed an interest in psychic phenomena, it was always as a nonbeliever. At Doyle's suggestion, Houdini attended eight séances with the attractive young French medium, Eva C. (Marthe Béraud). Both Professor Charles Richet and Baron Schrenck-Notzing had witnessed the materialization of the spirit of her guide, "Bien Boa," a Brahman Hindu who claimed to have lived 300 years ago.

In 1920, Eva C was invited to England by the Society of Psychical Research (S.P.R.). She spent two months in London giving forty séances for the society "Of the London work, in his *Thirty Years of Psychical Research* (1923), Richet states: "The official reports of the séances lead to very distinct inferences; it seems that though the external conditions were unfavorable to success, some results were very clear and that it is impossible to refer the phenomena to fraud."[8]

When members of the S.P.R. came to no conclusion, Dr. Richet was furious. How could they even suggest trickery regurgitation of cheese cloth? He wondered "How can masses of mobile substance, organized as hands, faces and drawings, be made to emerge from the esophagus or the stomach?"[9]

Naturally, Arthur Conan Doyle wanted a full account of Eva C.'s séance from his new friend. Houdini obliged by giving accounts of the séances in which he described the materializations as "highly interesting", but privately he stated that he was " 'not in any way convinced by the demonstrations', attributing the medium's feats to regurgitation and described the ectoplasm that issued from her body as nothing more than inflated rubber." [10]

While Houdini feigned interest to gain entrance to the séance room, Doyle was a sincere believer ever since the death of his son, Kingsley. Several mediums had brought through messages from Kingsley and subsequently Sir Arthur became an ardent Spiritualist. His wife, Lady Jean Conan Doyle, was also interested and developed her own mediumship. When Houdini heard of Doyle's communication with his dead son, Kingley, and Jean Conan Doyle's mediumship, he showed an interest. Conan Doyle was flattered, so when the couple saw the genuine devotion Houdini had for his deceased mother, Lady Conan Doyle offered her services.

He took Lady Doyle up on her kind offer when the Doyles visited the Houdinis in Atlantic City on June 18, 1922. There are many ways of contacting the spirits. Some mediums do so clairvoyantly, others through trance, and some like Lady Conan Doyle are most comfortable with automatic writing. Of the three methods, automatic writing is the riskiest, as the medium neither sees nor hears the spirit, but rather the entity seizes hold of the medium's hand in order to write messages. The messages can range from a Geraldine Cummins novel to pure gibberish.

Lady Doyle's communications from a spirit were well meaning, but they lacked the evidence that Houdini's sharp mind demanded:

Oh, my darling, my darling, thank God at last I am through. I've tried, oh, so often. Now I am happy. Of course, I want to talk to my boy, my own beloved boy.... My only shadow has been that my beloved one has not known how often I have been with him all the while I want him only to know that that I have bridged the gulf that is what I wanted — oh, so much. Now I can rest in peace.[11]

The basic problem was Cecilia Weiss did not know English and always spoke to her son in Yiddish. While Sir Arthur Conan Doyle found the pages that flowed from Lady Doyle's hand genuine, Harry remained unconvinced. He did not doubt the medium's sincerity, but he was skeptical of the spirit who claimed to be his mother's-especially when she addressed him as Harry; his mother had always called him Ehrich.

If Houdini had concerns, he kept them to himself. However, if he had voiced his doubts concerning Lady Conan Doyle's automatic writing. Her husband would have explained that sometimes spirits communicate mind to mind. Sometimes the medium's own consciousness may color the message. However, Houdini was too polite to criticize Lady Doyle's spirit communication.

Eventually Houdini came to regard mediums as clever conjurers and sought out the more celebrated mediums for the purpose of learning more about their tricks. He was particularly interested in the stage mediums- the Davenport brother and Anna Eva Fay. The Davenport Brothers were Ira Erastus Davenport (1839-1911) and William Henry

The Medium Who Baffled Houdini

Davenport (1841 – 1877). When their father, Buffalo New York policeman, heard of the mediumship of the Fox Sisters in Hydesville NY, he decided to try his own circle. Soon, they were in contact with the spirit of John King. In 1854 the 14-year-old and 16-year- old boys began their professional career. At John King's urging, their father rented a hall and put the young men on stage. While Kate and Maggie Fox communicated with ghosts by spirit raps, the Davenport Brothers used a cabinet for "spiritual manifestations." Both were tied to chairs and then the curtain to the cabinet was drawn. Musical instruments-violins, tambourines, and guitar were placed on the floor of the cabinet. Within minutes, the audience heard the sounds of the instruments being played by spirit hands. The boys traveled throughout the United States, and in 1864 they sailed for England. A success in both the United States and abroad, they continued until the death of William in 1877. Years later Harry Houdini visited Ira at his home in Mayville, New York. In 1924 Houdini included a chapter on the Davenports in his book, *A Magician Among the Spirits*. He also reproduced a letter from Ira claiming in regard to the brothers' performances "We never in public affirmed our belief in Spiritualism." [12]

Another medium who Houdini consulted was Anna Eva Fay (1855-1927). This noted American medium produced phenomena quite similar to that of the Davenport brothers. Born as Anna Eva Heathman in Southington, Ohio, she toured the United States and England billed as "The Indescribable Phenomenon." In 1874 she caught the attention of Sir William Crookes, the noted physicist, when she performed her mediumship act at the Crystal Palace in London. He was success both here and abroad, they continued until the death of William Davenport in 1877 so impressed by her "act," that he invited her to his laboratory for tests. In February of 1875, under laboratory conditions, Fay was able to move a music box across the room and ring a bell while holding two electrodes connected to a galvanometer in an adjoining room, which indicated any variation in the medium's grip. Impressed, Crookes published a favorable account of the experiment the medium (March 12, 1875). [13]

As early as 1912, Houdini wrote to Anna Eva Fay, and continued a professional correspondence until his death. "It became progressively more personal over the years, with Houdini sometimes expressing difficulty reading Anna's tortured handwriting, a situation he diplomatically covered by asking for clarifications of her meanings."[14] Fay was also interested in other professionals and kept in contact with many mediums in the area. When Houdini's name was mentioned unkindly, she remained loyal to her friend: "Still involved with local mediums, Anna described in one letter to Houdini that when she had ten mediums to dinner, she had defended him and his public attacks on fraudulent mediums against the complaints of her guests, and tried, unsuccessfully to convince them that he was actually on their side." [15]

When Harry Houdini finally met Anna Eva Fay, they became fast friends. Both were charismatic performers not adverse to mixing mediumship with magic. According to her grandson, David H Pingree, Anna Eva Fay met Harry Houdini in 1924. "In July 1924 (after retiring due to an on-stage wrist injury), she welcomed Houdini, who she befriended and collaborated with. She revealed the tricks/secrets, and even how she overcame Crookes' "electricity test"-considered impossible."[16]

Houdini considered Mrs. Fay "the cleverest medium of the world" according to his biographer, Ken Silverman. The clever Anna Eva Fay was part medium, part charlatan-She seems to have started out as a genuine medium, trained in Spiritualist circles in her youth. During World War I she performed across the United States answering questions such as "Is my boy safe?" and "When will the war end?" At first she stated World War I would end on December 18, 1915. She later revised her prophecy in Toledo in 1917. She said, "America will be the world's greatest nation. All the blooded stock of Europe is being slaughtered. Ten years from now, the world will look to America for its leaders." [17]

While her prophecies had a ring of truth to them, her physical mediumship seems to have been aided by mechanical hands. British Spiritualist, J. Hewat Mc Kenzie took in one of Anna Eva Fay's stage performances. "Afterwards, he stated confidently that a small pair of materialized and apparently jointless arms, resembling those of a monkey protruded from her chest, enabling her to do all of the cabinet manifestations."[18] Anna had no comment.

Anna Eva Fay did talk to Harry Houdini on their July 9, 1924, for five hours. The magician summarized their first meeting in eight pages of notes. "Anna described how, in her early years, she would play up to rich men, claim that her husband was impotent and she had a need only they could satisfy, suggesting various things, then at the right moment would walk away from them with her pockets full of gold."[19] After hearing the last comment, the moral magician was even more determined to stamp out the plague of mediumship sweeping the country. When Harry Houdini walked into the séance room at 10 Lime Street on July 23, 1924, he was convinced Margery Crandon was a clever fake medium-just like Anna Eva Fay. All he wanted to know was how Margery Crandon pulled off her "act."

End Notes

1. http://www.pbs.org/wgbh/amex/houdini/sfeature/margery1.html.
2. http://en.wikipedia.org/wiki/Jean_Eug%C3%A8ne_Robert Houdinhis.
3. *The Secret Life of Houdini*, William Kaloush and Larry Sloman, Atria Books, New York, NY 2006, page 294.
4. Ibid., page 340.
5. Ibid., page 349.
6. Ibid., page 362.
7. *The Man Who Created Sherlock Holmes,* Andrew Lycett, Free Press, New York, NY, page 407
8. http://www.answers.com/topic/eva-c.
9. *The Man Who Created Sherlock Holmes*, op. cit., page 408.
10. http://www.answers.com/topic/eva-c.
11. http://skeptoid.com/episodes/4430.
12. http://en.wikipedia.org/wiki/Davenport_Brothers"
13. The Indescribable Phenomenon, Barry H. Wiley, Hermetic Press, Seattle WA, 2007, page 177-179
14. Ibid., page 307.
15 Ibid. page 309.
16. http://genforum.genealogy.com/pingree/messages/87.html.
17. *The Indescribable Phenomenon*, op. cit., page 304.
18. Ibid., page 299.
19. Ibid., page 312.

Chapter 10

Magician Meets Medium

Margery, Boston Medium, Passes all Psychic Tests **New York Times**

"She is a fraud, a total fraud! "thought Houdini as he glanced at the bold print of the morning headlines. For weeks, newspaper headlines proclaimed "Margery, the Boston Medium Passes All Tests." Other papers enlarged upon the conservative "New York Times, "Boston Medium Baffles Experts," "Psychic Power of Margery Established, "and finally" Houdini the Magician Stumped." [1]

Appalled by the last headline and the reports that the Scientific American Committee was about to award Margery Crandon the $5,000 prize for genuine psychic phenomena, Houdini swiftly went into action and gained a place on the committee. There was no way the Great Houdini was going to let Margery steal the show or to let Malcolm Bird gain an upper hand. Houdini didn't have much faith in Bird whom he viewed as too friendly an observer. The researcher, known his champagne tastes, often enjoyed a fine meal and first-class- liquor and wine at the Crandon's dinner table. "Bird has even been their over-night guest- how cozy!" thought Houdini.

"No wonder he wrote such a glowing report in *Scientific America.* Houdini reflected, as he quickly dismissed Malcolm Bird's article in *Scientific America.* Houdini had little respect for Malcolm Bird and viewed him an amateur investigator-naive enough to endorse Margery Crandon before the committee had come to a decision. Houdini was not alone in his objections to Bird's easy-chair observations. The committee agreed to put Margery to the test.

Houdini trusted no one on the Scientific American committee. "What do these scientist s know about conjuring? Houdini mused. He had seen it and had total confidence in his ability to detect fraud in the séance room. He had done so many times in the past when he attended séances in disguise. Even Cecil Cook, a trumpet medium, who like Margery preferred to work in the dark, was surprised by a well-timed flashlight. To Houdini's delight, Cook was caught with a trumpet in his mouth.

As usual, Houdini was taking no chances. He arranged a meeting with famed stage medium Anna Eva Fay- only days before the séance to gather information on mediumship tricks. The magician even put a tight rubber bandage around his calf that day to make his leg more sensitive to the touch before the séance, just in case Margery's limb slipped out of position. "Nothing gets by the Great Houdini," he thought. Still he needed an ace up his sleeve in the form of a foolproof cabinet he had worked on with his assistance, Jim. Collins. "That will fix Margery," he thought. Evidently, failure was not a word in Houdini's vocabulary.

While Houdini was meeting with Anna Eva Fay, Margery was conducting séances for the other committee members: "During the séance on July 11th attended by committee members Dr. Daniel Comstock, Hereward Carrington, and Carrington's friend, magician Fred Keating Walter, manifested lights, rang the bell box, and then caused Margery's breasts to glow sporadically. He also took time to compose a little ditty about Houdini: "Harry Houdini, he sure is sheeny. A man with a crook in his shoes. Says he to Walter.' I'll lead him to slaughter.' But says Walter perhaps I'll get you.' " [2]

During the next séance, July 13, Walter rang the bell box on command: "The bell box now became the piece de la resistance of the Lime Street séance room. On July 13, it was on the floor at Margery's left; hand and foot control were scrupulously maintained; and the illuminated plague was used. Walter in spite of all this rang the bell as pleased, and as requested giving a combination of loud and short rings for several of the
sitters." [3]

The séance room had become a virtual "psychic circus." "The bell rang, the tambourine was shaken in mid-air, the megaphone was used for talking and whistling, a psychic dog barked and was represented by Walter to be a pet that Laura C lost several years ago, a brilliant light shone brilliantly on the tambourine, and Margery's keen laughter at all this was heard- all at the same time!" [4]

In all Margery had given fifty séances in which she had contacted Walter and other spirits for the scientists. Still she felt a curious combination of excitement and nerves on the morning of July 23, 1924. She woke up with a queen-size case of the jitters and an upset stomach. "She has been merrily throwing up," observed her husband.

Dr. Crandon wrote to Sir Arthur Conan Doyle who had recommended Margery to the committee concerning his wife. She was both excited about the séance and at the same time dreaded going into a deep trance. She sensed a battle brewing. Suddenly, the prospect of doing a séance seemed as inviting as swimming through a pool of crocodiles.

Margery's instinct were correct. Two worlds were about to collide when Harry Houdini walked into her séance room the evening of July 23, 1924. The magician and the medium came from different backgrounds. Houdini was largely self-educated, while Margery, on the other hand, was married to a Harvard educated physician. Houdini was Jewish; Margery, was a Christian. Their biggest difference was their intentions-which were wider apart than the shores of the Charles River. Houdini was a performer who commanded huge fees for his services. Margery, on the other hand, took no money for her séances. She had even refused to accept the $5, 000 dollar prize offered by *Scientific American*. While Harry Houdini was a master of illusion; Margery Crandon was a genuine medium. She gave up control completely to her spirit guide Walter-who, by the way, remained supremely confident in her abilities. He told his sister not to worry -"Houdini's number is up." Walter was not afraid of the self-promotion.

At age fifty, the magician was reviving his career with a public crusade against Spiritualists. Margery had no such complaint with the magician or any other researcher. She had begun her mediumship on a whim, and preferred to remain anonymous-known only as Medium Margery to the public. With all the publicity, it became impossible to keep her identity a secret. All it took was one zealous reporter to trail the committee member's car right to number 10 Lime Street and Mrs. Le Roi Crandon. By August Crandons' secret was revealed. On August 10, 1924, the New York Times ran the headline: "Margery is Identified: Boston Psychic Medium is the Wife of Dr. Le Roi G. Crandon."

Matters went from bad to worse when the press discovered her identity. "Now the pressure was really on," thought Margery. No wonder she seemed nervous as a mouse in the shadow of a hungry cat.

The Medium Who Baffled Houdini

Maybe that was why she and Dr. Crandon were not getting along. Or had another pretty nurse who succumbed to Dr. Crandon's advances? If so, Margery was too much a lady to make a scene. In the past, even amid rumors of her husband's infidelities, Margery and Dr. Crandon had managed to pull off united front in public. Now, the dour doctor seemed oblivious to his wife's feelings. Things had deteriorated to the point where Dr. Crandon was only attentive to his wife after a good séance.

Lately, Margery hadn't been paying too much attention to her husband either. Someone else was on her mind-Dr. Hereward, the noted English researcher. He believed in Margery more than her husband. If the rumors were true, the distinguished researcher was more than a friend to the medium. For weeks now the couple kept their distance from each other. Those closest to them whispered "They are not getting on."

Tongues really wagged when Hereward Carrington moved into the Crandons' spare bedroom. Rumors of an affair between the Margery and Carrington began to circulate- gossip neither bothered to deny. While Carrington remained discreet, Margery told everyone who would listen that Hereward Carrington had asked to sell the family home which was in her name and to run away with him to Egypt. As romantic as the idea was, Margery remained at 10 Lime Street. She still had a twelve year old son to think about.

Hereward Carrington would not attend the July séances, because he found Houdini's presence objectionable. Margery was jittery around the magician. However, she knew how to put on a happy face, in order to concentrate on the séance. There were several things at hand. The evening of the first séance with Houdini in the audience, Margery chose her dressing gown with great care. All she ever wore to a séance was a loose kimono, slippers, and silk stockings. The medium's seductive figure, blonde hair and blue eyes made it difficult for the investigators- all male-to keep their minds on science. As Dr. Prince had aptly noted it if he wished to be taken seriously as a psychic researcher, he had "to avoid falling in love with the medium."

Margery Crandon was used to men falling in love with her. She knew she had a gorgeous figure, and was not shy about opening her dressing gown to be being photographed partially nude during a séance.

"It is all for science", she told critics, "How else could they get a picture of ectoplasm coming out of my vagina?"

The medium's candor and outgoing nature appealed to both men and woman. She possessed that rare ability to make people feel unique as she focused her considerable charm on them. Houdini had been warned beforehand that she might try to "vamp" him.

When Margery looked into Houdini's dark eyes, he took care to reveal nothing. She was also careful not to be swayed by Houdini's magnetic eyes known to hypnotize theatre audiences. "Houdini finds me attractive," Margery sensed immediately, "but he doesn't believe in me. " In no way was she fooled by the magician's frank stare or polite patter. She just smiled visualizing Houdini's face when he saw the trumpet sail through the air. "Too bad I am going to miss his expression when he finds out I am real thing, "the trance medium thought to herself.

July 23, 1924, the day of séance turned out to be one of the hottest recorded in Boston. The evening temperatures were in the high eighties when Houdini arrived at the Lime Street residence, accompanied by O.D. Munn, editor of "Scientific American." The two paid scant attention to the heat, as they trudged up the four floors to the séance room. They were anxious to observe the psychic accomplishments of the alluring 36-year-old flapper known for her bewitching blue eyes.

Harry Houdini, sensed an uneasy energy present in the room when he entered the fourth floor library of the Crandons' home. However, if Margery was nervous, she was careful to conceal it. She greeted him with her characteristic warmth. "I have been hearing some very nice things about you lately, so I am glad to able to say I know the Great Houdini." He smiled, but avoided the blue eyes of his hostess.

Margery appeared as light-hearted. For the séance portion of the evening, Margery wore nothing more than a flimsy negligee. If her séance outfit was too sensual for the straight-laced Houdini, took pains not to show his reaction. A master of misdirection, he was determined to keep his mind clear of any seductive trap or spell Margery might try to cast over him. He instinctively did not trust the medium, and thought her husband was probably the mastermind behind the charade. All Houdini had on his mind when he entered the séance room was how Margery Crandon managed to fool the Harvard and M.I.T. scientists. He believed she was an attractive fake just like Anna Eva Fay.

The Medium Who Baffled Houdini

As for Malcolm Bird, the dislike was mutual. He considered Houdini's presence on the Scientific American committee, a grave error. "Who does he think he is, thought Mr. Bird, insisting on being on our committee?" He implored Orson D. Munn, owner of *Scientific America* to keep Houdini in line. Munn agreed to be at Margery's side for all of the five séances in which Houdini was present. Bird simply did not trust Houdini. As far Bird was concerned Houdini was only there to find fault and discredit the medium. "All Houdini is looking for is publicity," thought Bird. "Well he is not going to hurt Margery for his own gain!"

Magic was definitely not in the air the evening of July 23, 1924, when Harry Houdini took his place in the circle. Margery, deeply sensitive, felt the sting of negative energy immediately. She kept her opinion to herself, noting that Houdini's aura registered the opposite energy of his spoken word. If there was one thing Margery was keenly aware of, it was vibrations. They could make or break a séance. The right vibrations would heighten the atmosphere to aid the production of physical phenomena. Negative energy, on the other hand, was deadly. Under hostile conditions the table would remain still and the trumpet would not budge an inch.

Margery knew she had her work cut out for her. If the séance was to be a success, the vibrations had to be raised. Like most mediums, she had learned how to ignore criticism and focus on positive energy. She did her best to be charming and listened carefully to Houdini. If the beautiful medium was at all ill at ease, she didn't show it. She remained extremely pleasant to him all evening.

For his part, Houdini was cordial to Margery. He had visited her home earlier in the day when he was invited to inspect the séance room. He reported that he found nothing amiss. He saw no trapdoors, invisible wires, or false bottoms. The magician was satisfied with the inspection, and he was keen to observe the séance.

The circle assembled for that evening included Margery and Dr. Crandon, Malcolm Bird, Mr. Munn, Mr. Conan, and Houdini. As customary it was conducted in pitch darkness. Carrington was not present. It was reported that he had deliberately left town to avoid being in the same room with Houdini. Soon Walter's voice was heard clearly. "'Have Houdini tell me where to throw it,' the voice had commanded.

"'Toward me,' answered Houdini, whereupon the megaphone instantly crashed to the ground in front of him.",$_5$ Walter then instructed Bird to take his place in the doorway; and almost before Bird could comply, cabinet was thrown violently on its back, with no preliminaries; Margery's chair was pushed forward as usual when this had happened before.[6] Apparently Walter was acting out.

Next an illuminated plaque was placed on the table. "Houdini in the best place for observation, raising, lowering, oscillations, movements back and forth. Ultimately it skewed around at an angle. One movement stood out above all others, the plaque rising slightly at one end and at least eight inches at other, and standing for an instant at an angle estimated by Bird as perhaps sixty degrees."[7] Houdini, Bird, and Munn all signed a sword statements to the veracity of these events.

Privately, Houdini told Munn, Conan, and Bird on their ride home: "Well gentlemen, I've got her. All fraud every bit of it. One more sitting and I will be able to expose every bit of it. But one thing puzzles me-I don't see how she did that megaphone trick." [8] Obviously, Margery had stumped Houdini with the trumpet levitation.

On the next evening of July 24th, the séance was scheduled for 8:40 p.m. at Dr. Comstock's apartment at 535 Beacon Street. Margery sat on the left of Houdini, on his left was O. D Munn, then Dr. Crandon, and then Bird. Just outside the circle sat Dr. Comstock and Miss Wood. By 9:00 the séance was in full swing accounting to the official transcript:

> 9:00: Bird says the right hand wing of the cabinet moved an inch or two toward Margery Houdini says something touched my knee.
>
> At the same time Walter's remark was "Ha Ha Houdini
>
> 9:02: Megaphone moved and the cabinet shivered, says Bird. Cabinet opened up widely at the right [9]

Houdini then observed the cabinet shaking, and the megaphone sliding across the floor. He verified that the table was up on two legs and falling over him. At 10:30 Walter concluded the séance by ringing the bell box:

> 10:30: The contact apparatus rang one long peal. All controls reported perfect as previously. Half a minute later another ring. He (Walter) then asked Munn how many times he should ring

it. Munn said five. One, two, three, four, five. He ten said said, "good night."[10]

Everyone present signed the report. Houdini and Munn looking out for their own interest added the postscript that 'in event of publication the document should be published in full.

Houdini would later allege that Margery rang the bell box which was placed under Houdini's chair with her left foot during the séance. This would seem an unlikely explanation as Houdini had his foot firmly blocking hers. Besides with his "sensitive" leg, how could the conjurer not have felt pressure if the medium moved some much as an inch during the séance. Obviously, Margery had stumped Houdini with the trumpet levitation. Disgusted, Bird later challenged Houdini with this wry remark: "Asked by the audience at Boston Symphony Hall, why he didn't expose her on the spot, he must ignore the query- because there is no answer. And he poses as the great detector in the séance room!"[11]

End Notes

1. *Margery the Medium*, J. Malcolm Bird., Small, Maynard and Company, Boston, page 46.
2. *The Secret Life of Houdini*, William Kaloush and Larry Sloman, Atria Books, New York, NY 2006, page 415.
3. *Margery the Medium*, op cit., page 397.
4. Ibid., page 398.
5. http://www.historynet.com/mina-crandon-harry-houdini-the-medium-and-the-magician.htm
6. *Margery the Medium,* op. cit., page 409.
7. Ibid., page 410.
8. Ibid., page 413.
9. Ibid., page 414.
10. Ibid., page 416.
11. Ibid., page 424.

"Margery the Medium" turned out to be socialite, Mrs. Le Roi Crandon.

Walter Stinson, Margery's brother, who became her spirit guide.

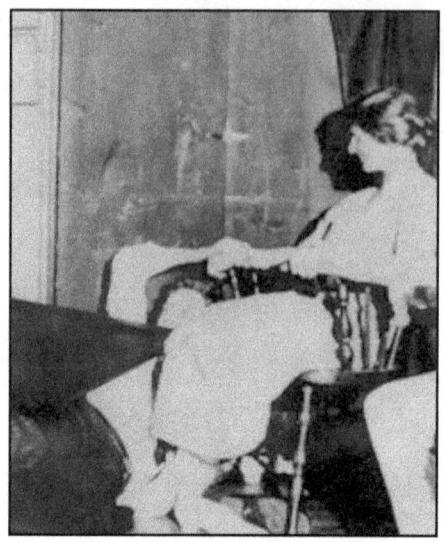

Margery Crandon is amused by the cabinet collapsing around Malcolm Bird.

Medium Margery Crandon, surrounded by O.D. Munn, editor of *Scientific American*, J. Malcolm Bird, and Harry Houdini, Courtesy of Library of Congress.

Researcher, Hereward Carrington   Dr. Daniel F. Comstock

Dr. Walter Franklin Prince   Dr. William McDougall

Margery in trance. Notice the ectoplasm voice box on her right shoulder.

Margery in trance--a third hand coming out from beneath her skirt.

Harry Houdini in his "Margie Box." Courtesy Library of Congress.

Sir Arthur Conan Doyle

MARGERY GENUINE, SAYS CONAN DOYLE; HE SCORES HOUDINI

MEDIUM AND HER NEW CHAMPION

MRS. MINA CRANDON
Who, as Margery, is Storm Centre in Psychic Controversy

SIR ARTHUR CONAN DOYLE
Who Comes to Defense of Mrs. Crandon
(Bain News Service)

Margery Crandon with her husband, Dr. Le Roi Crandon.

Chapter 11

Walter Versus Houdini

The psychic does not refuse to sit in the cage made by Houdini for the committee, but she makes the reservation that she knows no precedent in psychic research where a medium has been so enclosed; she believes that such a closed cage gives little or no regard to the theory or experience of the psychic structure or mechanism. **Dr. Le Roi Crandon**

    Malcolm Bird was not the only person disgusted with Houdini's lack of integrity, Margery's spirit guide, Walter was furious with the magician turned psychic investigator. From now on the spirit planned to keep a few steps ahead of Houdini. It would be an easy task for him. After all, spirit guides exist on a higher plane- one which allows them a higher vantage point to readily see the future.

    Guides play an essential role in the séance room. Not only do they protect the medium during the séance, but they also act as a go between the two worlds. Spirit control is extremely important in trumpet mediumship which requires total darkness. Some mediums will not allow even a ray of light in the room, because light would destroy the delicate ectoplasm needed to lift the trumpet. Once a trumpet séance begins, no one is allowed to leave the room; and, under no circumstances, may a sitter touch a medium in trance. To do so could cause great harm to the medium, as the ectoplasm is attached to the medium's solar plexus. A sitter who disturbs the trance medium by shining a flashlight or even walking into the room, would cause the ectoplasm to painfully retract into the medium's solar plexus.

    Walter adhered to these ground rules--though on occasion, he did allow a red light. As with most trance mediums, Margery gave up control to her guide once she entered the cabinet. At that point sitting entranced in the cabinet, ectoplasm was drawn from all of Margery's orifices and formed into cords that attached to the trumpet. When Walter felt the vibrations were right, he began speaking through the trumpet.

The Medium Who Baffled Houdini

This type of mediumship is known as direct voice. The trumpet acts as a megaphone to project the spirit's voice within hearing range of all the sitters. In order to do so, the medium must be in deep trance and the room must be totally dark. Guides such as Walter come through to aid the medium. If conditions are right, objects such as jewelry, religious relics, or gems may be heard rattling down the trumpet. These "apports" are introduced by spirit helpers during the sitting.

Houdini scoffed at the thought of trumpet mediumship. He was sure that Margery's trance was a ruse and Walter's antics produced by fakery. He had little interest in what he believed to be bogus spirit guides. If he had bothered to study at the College of Psychic Sciences in London or read one of Dr. Crawford's books on mediumship, he would have known that once the trumpet is in the air, it is vitally important to remain receptive to spirit and keep the energy high. Doubt and negativity have no place in the séance circle.

The next series of séances were scheduled for August 25, 26, 27, and 1924. This time Walter was ready for Houdini. He knew the magician had little knowledge of mediumship, so the only way Houdini could discredit Margery would be through trickery. When it came to "the kid," Walter planned to pull no punches.

On August 25th the committee met at the Charlesgate Hotel in Boston. The city was in the throes of a heat wave with temperatures reaching 98 that afternoon. The hot weather did not help Houdini's mood. He was already on the defensive when he arrived at the hotel. He decided that bring out his own cabinet-"a fraud-proof cage." To her credit, Margery agreed to use Houdini's cabinet. Dr. Crandon, on the other hand, had reservations, adding this statement to the record: "The psychic does not refuse to sit in the cage made by Houdini for the committee, but she makes the reservation that she knows no precedent in psychic research where a medium has been so enclosed; she believes that such a closed cage gives little or no regard to the theory or experience of the psychic structure or mechanism."

Houdini wasn't pleased by Crandon's remarks, but he let it pass. First, he didn't believe any psychic structure was moving the trumpet. Dr. Crandon, well versed in parapsychology, believed otherwise. He had witnessed ectoplasmic structures in the shape of cords lift the trumpet to act as a megaphone to amplify the voices of spirit.

Thus, by stating in advance that the "closed cage gives little or no regard to the theory or experience of the psychic structure or mechanism." Crandon was being cautious. If Margery was unable to extrude the ectoplasm necessary to lift the trumpet, or if the ectoplasm became stuck in the cabinet, Dr. Crandon had paved a way for Margery to save face. Dr. Crandon need not have been concerned. Margery had an ally on her side -her guide, Walter Stinson.

Dr. Crandon who already had little faith in Houdini, stipulated that both Margery and Houdini also had to sit in whatever mechanical control the magician fashioned. Crandon, who envisioned "mechanical control" to mean handcuffs or ropes, was appalled by the cage Houdini brought in-and only one cage at that. "Obviously," thought Dr. Crandon, "Houdini has no intention of keeping his promise to be in the same apparatus as Margery during the séance. "

Earlier in the morning of August 25, Jim Collin, Houdini's assistant, arrived to set the wood cage up in Comstock's apartment. Collins followed Houdini's instructions with precision. He was careful to fit the lid with staples, and the clasps and padlocks just as the Boss had told him. "There was no way that bloody lady is going to stand up in this cabinet," he thought as he double-checked his work. Jim was a talented carpenter and mechanic who invented the Chinese Water Torture Cell. He was always the one to tie the knots for the magician before he was lowered into the cell. Houdini trusted no assistant more than Collins. Houdini never failed to remember his assistant's birthday or Christmas. When he made a promise to his employer, the English assistant followed orders- no questions asked. After all Houdini was the Boss. "There is one thing you got to remember about Mister oudidni, in his last years, for 'im, the truth was bloody well wanted what 'e wanted it to be."[1]

Just in case, someone became nosey, neither the committee members nor Dr. Crandon were allowed to examine the cabinet- a most peculiar condition. However, "as a condition of mechanical control, F.H. (Friend Husband) specified that Margery should be sitting surrounded only by friends, and using the apparatus so provided. The idea was to get Walter's assurance that the controlling devices were satisfactory to him and not unsatisfactory to him, and they were comfortable to her."[2] Margery cheerfully got into the cage and the wooded top was fastened down. Only then did Houdini withdraw from the room.

Margery and her small circle of friends sat while the committee members and assistants waited in another room. The friendly circle served as a battery for the medium. In about half an hour, Margery went into a deep trance. Before long, Walter came through with his characteristic whistle and said everything was okay for the committee members to enter.

Houdini and the rest of the Scientific America committee were called into the séance room. Next, according to Malcolm Bird, " Shortly after the formal committee sitting started , a violent noise was heard, on turning on the light the entire top of Margery's cage was open, the diagonal doors having been thrown back."[3] Apparently, Houdini's "fraud-proof cage" was not spirit-proof. Houdini quickly said, "Anyone could throw it open using their shoulders."

Walter, after a few curt words, demanded another sitting with Margery's friends to clear the negative atmosphere. Fifteen minutes later, Walter was ready for the committee members and Houdini and the others were summoned. Walter quickly got to the point: "Houdini, have you got the mark just right?" When Dr. Comstock demanded to know what Walter meant, Walter replied: "Comstock, you take that box into white light and examine it, and report back. You'll see fast enough what I mean."[4]

Dr. Comstock examined the bell box and found an eraser stuck between the contact boards which would make it difficult to ring the bell-a phenomenon that occurred regularly in Margery's séance room. Houdini immediately volunteered, "I didn't do it!" No one except Houdini would have had the opportunity to tamper with the bell box, as he had kept his eyes on the cage until the lid had been fastened.

With such shenanigans, it is surprising that the Crandons even agreed to another séance on August 26. Suspicions ran high. The committee members insisted that the top of the cage be properly secured. The next morning Houdini and his assistant Jim Collins added paddocks and staples to secure the top of the cabinet.

Everyone was on edge--even Harry Houdini. When Mr. Conant, an employee of Dr. Comstock who had a key to the apartment, let himself in without ringing the bell, Houdini became paranoid. He accused the employee of spying and demanded Conant be fired. The accusation was so ridiculous, everyone just laughed. Why was the usually composed magician so angry? Was it just a case of nerves or had Houdini another trick up his sleeve?

Malcolm Bird was especially suspicious. "The episode reinforces the strong presumption already existing that there was something radically wrong about the 'fraud-proof' cage; and it throws strong light upon Houdini's penchant for promiscuous suspicions and charges."[5] Tension ran high on both sides. Neither Bird nor the Crandons trusted Houdini, and the other committee members were equally wary.

To insure that Margery was not concealing any hidden paraphernalia, she was thoroughly frisked by Miss McManama, the stenographer. Margery then proceeded directly to the séance room which add been meticulously searched by Dr. Comstock except for one item- the séance cage. Houdini refused to let anyone touch his invention.

Margery was then seated in the cage with three portholes- one for her head and two for her arms. Thus secured, Houdini admonished Dr. Prince several times, "Do not relinquish Margery's hands on any account." Apprehensive, Margery shot back, "If you are not sure everything is alright why don't you search me again and search this cage?"[6]

"No," said Houdini "Let's get started." Margery quickly entered trance and Walter took over. "He immediately asserted that there was a ruler in the cage with the psychic, under the cushion on which her feet rested; by innuendo, rather than explicitly, he charged Houdini of having put it there; he swore fearfully at Houdini, called down curses on his head, and applied opprobrious epithets to him."[7] Houdini who objected to Walter calling him "a son of a bitch," shouted out "My dear sainted mother was married to my father," and denied having any knowledge of the ruler.

Dr. Comstock restored order in the room by reminding Walter that anyone could have left a ruler in the cage. Collins, Houdini's assistant who had assembled the cage, was then called in. He testified that he had left no ruler in the cage. There was nothing left to do, but to open the cage and search for the ruler. There, exactly in the spot Walter had designated, was a carpenter's seven- inch folding ruler. Only Collins and Houdini had had access to the cabinet and both the motive and opportunity to plant the ruler. Each swore on his mother's grave that they did not.

August 27 was another hot, muggy day. Margery sat for trance in the airless cabinet, but without any success. Walter did not make an appearance. All Margery could do was sit in the hot cabinet for over an hour, while the committee members argued about the best method of control. For the moment Houdini had the upper hand. Then Dr. Comstock laid down the law. "All through these sittings you had tried to get us to refer to that cage in the records as the committee's, and insisting that it isn't yours. But you have refused to let us examine it and behaved in other ways as if the cage were yours. Now you must choose. If it is the committee's, it stays here for future use."[8] Houdini's response was to bring the cabinet back to New York.

Not surprised by the magician's hasty action, Bird agreed with Walter who had charged Houdini with fraud. Bird noted, "His (Houdini's) conduct from beginning to end was that of one who was firmly committed to the proposition psychic phenomena cannot and must not be; and who is determined to establish this thesis by any means possible."[9]

Houdini's lack of ethics was confirmed in 1959 when William Lindsay Gresham published Jim Collin's confession: "Years later, when the Self-Liberator (Houdini) was dead, Jim Collins (Houdini's assistant) was asked about the mysterious ruler. Collins smiled wryly. 'I chucked it in the box meself. The boss told me to do it. He wanted to fix her good.'"[10]

End Notes

1. *Houdini: The man Who Walked Through Walls*, William Lindsay, Gresham, Manor Books, New York, NY, 1975, page 219.
2. *Margery the Medium*, J. Malcolm Bird., Small, Maynard and Company, Boston, page 428.
3. Ibid., pages 428-9.
4. Ibid., page 430.
5. Ibid., page 431.
6. Ibid., page 431.
7. Ibid, page 433.
8. Ibid., page 435.
9. Ibid., page 436.
10. *Houdini: The man Who Walked Through Walls*, op. cite. page 219.

Chapter 12

"J.B. Rhine is an Ass"

We have only begun to fight and shall keep it up until their skins or ours are nailed to the wall. **Dr. Le Roi Crandon**

Unfortunately, Jim Collins' confession came many years later--too late to undo the damage that had been done to Margery's reputation. Even though, she had worked hard to prove herself to serious researchers in the United States and abroad, her mediumship was now under a cloud of suspicion. Researchers remained divided. British investigators, Sir Arthur Conan Doyle and Arthur Findley remained impressed by her trumpet séances, while Dr. Joseph B. Rhine dismissed her séances as hocus-pocus. When J.B. Rhine had submitted a damning report to the Journal of Abnormal and Social Psychology, denouncing Margery's mediumship, Doyle rushed to the medium's defense by placing an advertisement in Boston papers which bluntly stated, "J.B. Rhine is an ass."

Margery Crandon certainly inspired loyalty in her followers. She also made a strong impression on scientists at Harvard University. The faithful believed that her only flaw lie in her miscalculation of Houdini. She simply had not considered the possibility that the noted magician would stoop to trickery to discredit her mediumship. By the end of the summer of 1924, relations between Harry Houdini and both Crandons reached an all- time low.

Houdini was not in the least concerned. He was on a crusade to rid the world of those who prey on the grief-stricken. He had nothing but contempt for Margery, Dr. Crandon, and Malcolm Bird. To make his point, Houdini had printed at his own expense a pamphlet entitled "A Magician Among the Spirits. When it came out in November 1924, Houdini described Margery's trumpet mediumship as "the slickest ruse I have ever seen."

He literally attributed all of her phenomena to deception and misdirection. For instance, his explanation of how the trumpet floated

The Medium Who Baffled Houdini

in the air was "With her right hand she tilted the corner of the cabinet enough to get her free foot under it, then picking up the megaphone she placed it on her head, dunce-cap fashion. Then she threw the cabinet over with her right foot. As she did so I distinctly felt her body give and sway as though she had made a vigorous lunge."[1] Houdini neglected to mention that medium was in a dead trance all the time these calculated actions occurred.

Houdini had also invented stories about another medium, Anna Eva Faye in his pamphlet *Magician Among Spirits*. He claimed that Anna had revealed her tricks to him; however Faye's biographer, Barry Wiley dismisses this as "pure fantasy." [2] When Anna Eva Faye died of heart disease on May 12, 1927, at the age of 76, she took her secrets with her.

Margery's supporters viewed *Magician Among the Spirits* as an act of desperation by an author who would stoop to fantasy to discredit mediums. .Boston fans were especially appalled by the publication. When his pamphlet did not deter Margery's followers, Houdini staged a dramatic exposé of the medium at Symphony Hall in Boston. The Crandons then pleaded their cause before an audience at Boston's Jordan Hall. By February 1925, they refused to have any more meetings with Harry Houdini. Furious at Houdini's insults to the couple's integrity, Dr. Crandon vowed, "We have only begun to fight and shall keep it up until their skins or ours are nailed to the wall." [3]

The magician, who enjoyed publicity, was not deterred by Crandon's wrath. He continued the battle by assembling a Broadway show which featured an exposé of medium Margery. He even included a bell box similar to the one used in Margery's séances. While the show was riddled with half-truths, it made for popular entertainment.

Houdini's fans especially liked his last act, "Do the Dead Come Back? "which many considered worth the price of the ticket. The show opened late in 1925 to standing room only crowds. As part of the act, Houdini offered $10,000 to any medium who could produce physical phenomena that Houdini could not reproduce or explain by nature. Few mediums and psychics took the bait. However, those that did were ill-prepared for the veteran magician and were soon booed off the stage.

One of Houdini's last earthly deeds was a crusade in Congress to ban mediums. The hearings took place in February and May of 1926, in a hall packed with psychics and mediums.

Sadly, Houdini viewed spirit mediums as criminals. Spiritualists, the leading organization for mediums, on the other hand, stood by the first tenet of Spiritualism that states "There is no death and there are no dead. " Spiritualist view mediumship as God-given gift to be used for the purpose of proving the continuity of life. Tension ran high on both sides. For instance, the Reverend H.P. Strack, secretary of the National Spiritualist Association of Churches, stated he was surprised that anyone would heed the words of a "pronounced atheist and infidel."[4]

After several such attacks on his character, Harry Houdini put Bess, his wife of 32 years, on the stand. With typical Houdini showmanship, he began question her.

Houdini: "Outside of my great mother, Mrs. Houdini has been my greatest friend.

Have I ever shown any traces of being crazy unless it was about you?"

Bess: "No."

Houdini: "Am I brutal to you or vile?"

Bess: "No"

Houdini "Am I a good boy?"

Bess: "Yes."

With the last answer, the hearing room broke out in applause. [5]

However, Congress needed more than theatrics to pass the bill. After the hearings, Houdini even tried to get his journalist friend, Walter Lippman, who had been assistant to the Secretary of during War in World War I, involved. He wrote back, "Sorry to tell you I have heard on rather good authority that they do hold séances in the White House and am looking for further proof regarding same. This of course in strict confidence." [6]

In the end, the bill did not go through. Spiritualists, mediums, and clairvoyants in the United States could now sleep soundly through the night. Not unlike the Spiritualists, Houdini believed he had a mission. He viewed ridding the world of fraudulent mediums as a sacred charge and was willing to spend $40,000 a year from his own pocket to accomplish the task. He wrote researcher Harry Price, a fellow skeptic: "I believe the work I am doing is the greatest humanitarian achievement of my life." As Houdini explained to one reporter, "I have spent many hours on the stage and public forum, but now I am helping to alleviate the years of worry that is driving many to the brink of insanity by their inordinate desire to communicate with the dead." [7]

Life seemed to be going well for the famous magician. At age 52, Harry Houdini was looking forward to retirement with his wife. He had just been talking about buying property in Los Angeles. When he did retire from the stage, he planned to "tour California and take his fight against the spooks and their accomplices to the smaller towns" [8] However, just as the aging magician was considering retirement, Walter's prediction came true- "Houdini's number was up." Harry Houdini died from a ruptured appendix on Halloween, 1926.

Houdini will always be remembered as American's greatest magician. However, for Spiritualists, he was their worst enemy- a skeptic who would never be convinced of spirit communication. Even when he saw the trumpet float through the air and conversed with the lively intelligence known as Walter, he refused to believe his eyes or ears. Houdini remained a skeptic to the end.

Determined doubters, such as Houdini, always have a rational explanation for any physical phenomena. For example, he decided to contact the spirit of fellow magician, Lafayette. When he visited the great illusionist's grave in Edinburgh, Scotland, Houdini brought two pots of flowers. Placing the flowers in front of the deceased tombstone, Houdini solemnly intoned: "Lafayette, give us a sign you are here." Within seconds both pots were overturned. He quickly picked them up and set them upright. Apparently the spirit of the illusionist Lafayette sought Houdini's attentions, as the two pots crashed to the ground breaking into pieces. Did he take this as a sign from a spirit? Houdini later commented to friends, "It was all very strange, yet I do not attribute what happened to anything other than to the high wind which was blowing at the time." [9]

Even though Houdini would not be convinced by phenomena, there are skeptics who are willing to believe there could be some honest phenomena. Researchers such as Dr. William McDougall, Professor Henry Comas, and Dr. J. B. Rhine would fall into this second category of skeptics. These men of science seemed genuinely interested in Margery's mediumship initially. However, each required scientific proof of an imperfect science. Unlike physics whose laws can be calculated with great accuracy-as most genuine mediums are about 80-85 percent correct. Why? Doubt and distrust are common barriers to spirit communication. Also, a medium is an extremely sensitive person subject to individual peculiarities. Even mediums as talented as Margery Crandon can have an off day in which no phenomena is produced.

Finally, there are those who want to believe, but they are easily swayed by naysayers. Sadly, the majority of committee members fell into the last group. They wanted to believe, but were influenced by Houdini's negative view of Margery. Only Hereward Carrington championed Margery's mediumship: "As a result of more than forty sittings with Margery, I have arrived at the definite conclusion that genuine supernormal phenomena frequently occur. Many of the observed manifestations might well have been produced fraudulently however; there remains a number of instances when phenomena were produced and observed under practically perfect control." [10]

The other committee members did not share Carrington's enthusiasm, but they were not ready to declare Margery a fraud: "Margery's friends emphasize that Prince had sat ten times, Comstock, fifty-six times, and McDougall twenty-two times; and that none of the three were willing to stamp her as fraud or to say anything making it appear that he thinks she is a possible fraud."[11] Dr. Daniel Comstock's main objection was the darkness of the séance room: "My conclusion therefore is that rigid proof has not yet been furnished but that the case at present, is interesting and should be investigated further."[12]

Professor William McDougall concurred. He wanted more definite proof. As Malcolm Bird observed, "He is superstitious about the possibility of fraud; he lacks confidence in his own ability to say whether fraud has or has not been excluded. He leaves the séance room after a brilliant performance, granting freely that he knows no way for fraudulent production of what he had seen, that he can by no stretch of the imagination conceive such as way.[13] Professor McDougall withheld his validation any- unsure of an alternate explanation for the séance room phenomena.

As for Dr. Walter Franklin Prince, he seemed to have been the most uncertain. During one of the séance, ukulele went into Prince's lap and then pressed against his chest. He also felt something else which could have been an ectoplasmic rod or the psychic's foot. "He doesn't know it wasn't her foot, and hence that the ukulele manipulation means nothing," Bird explained.[4] Of the group, Prince seemed to be the most influenced by Harry Houdini, and like Houdini was anxious to conclude the investigation. Needlesstosay, Prince voted against Margery. Sir Arthur Conan Doyle, who was not a member of the committee, was appalled by their decision.

The noted writer pronounced "The phenomena are perhaps the best attested in the whole annals of psychic research." He was even more disgusted with his one-time friend, Harry Houdini Houdini's verdict, as expected, was harsh. In his letter to "Scientific American" dated August 28, 1924, Houdini accused Margery Crandon of manipulating her head, shoulders and left foot to produce physical phenomena: "Summing up my investigation of the five séances of Margery which took place July 23 and 24, August 25, 26, and 27, the fact that I deliberately caught her manipulating her head, shoulder, and left foot, the particulars of which I have handed to Mr. O. D. Munn. The blank séances, and incidences that took place at the last three tests: My decision is that everything that took place at the séances which I attended was a deliberate and conscious fraud, and that if the lady possesses any psychic power, at no time was the same proven at any of the above dated séances.[15]

In April, 1925, Scientific American's senior editor, O. D. Munn, ended their research into Margery Crandon: "The famous Margery case is over as far as Scientific American Psychic Investigation is concerned." Houdini was not Margery Crandon's only critic. Dr. J. B. Rhine, a pioneer in psychic research, claimed he was able to observe the use of luminous objects to fake séance phenomena and he even postulated that the medium suffered from a personality disorder.[16]

With all the attention, both Crandons even were more determined than ever to prove Margery's mediumship. The couple invited another investigator to their home, Eric Dingwall. In the summer. of 1924, Dingwall, a British investigator, had found Margery "a highly intelligent and charming young woman, exceedingly good natured, and possessed of a fund of good humor and courage which make her an ideal subject for investigation." [17]

Upon his return to 10 Lime Street, Dingwall was pleased to see Margery Crandon was still an ideal physical medium. While she slept peacefully in a deep trance, Dingwall witnessed an abundance of ectoplasm in the séance room. The milky substance emanated from within the medium's body, oozing out of her ears, mouth and her vagina. At the close of the séance, the ectoplasm returned naturally to its source. However, in the presence of light can be dangerous to the medium, as it can cause the ectoplasm to violently snap back into the body of the medium and in some cases may cause internal injuries. For this reason, most materialization séance are held in darkness. It is also advised that the séance room floor be kept spotless, to avoid debris which could enter the medium with the return of ectoplasm.

Eric Dingwall was thrilled when Walter promised to produce ectoplasm in full view in good red light. He observed a "long, thin 'tongue-like structure, issuing, not arrested, but issuing in slow motion from a slit in Margery's robe, under which she wore no clothes." [18] "It feels like cold, raw beef," Dingwall proclaimed when he was allowed to touch some of the ectoplasm under Walter's supervision. As for Margery, she made light of the whole investigation: "The first thing he (Dingwall) told me was to take off my clothes," she said with a twinkle in her eye. While Dingwall would have preferred the medium to wear black tights, that many European medium wore, Dr. Crandon vetoed the idea stating the tights might impede the ectoplasm. Perhaps this was why Margery wore the flimsiest of dressing gowns and silk stockings. At times, she was practically nude.[19]

On January 19, 1925, Eric Dingwall observed ectoplasm coming out of Margery left ear and mouth. He snapped a photograph that showed the white mass emanating. At times materializations formed from the ectoplasm: "In the next materialization, another hand appeared, this time moving sinuously, and occasionally startling against the cardboard plaque. Again the black mass was silhouetted in the darkness, lying inert until the squirming motion began, and from the central pulp one, two, three, four, five fingers were made to suddenly grow from out of the mass, some quickly, some slowly."[20]

As a result of this and other materializations, Dingwall was very much a believer in Margery's mediumship. He took time to write to a fellow researcher, Baron von Schrenck-Notzing, "It is the most beautiful case of telplasmic, telekinesis of which I am acquainted. One can freely touch the teleplasm (ectoplasm). The materialized hands are joined by cords to the medium's body, they seize objects and move these. "He noted all this occurred in good red light and "irreproachable control."[21]

With such good results, Dingwall was overjoyed and prepared to give a vigorous defense of Margery's mediumship at his lecture at Jordan Hall in Boston on January. What would have been a well-deserved victory for Dr. and Mrs. Crandon turned into a more, conservation lecture that remained neutral in tone. Why? The evening before Professor McDougall of Harvard made it a point to visit Eric Dingwall to point out the possibility of counterfeit mediumship.

At the end of Dingwall's formal report, he straddled the fence: "The mediumship remains one of the most remarkable in the history of psychical research. It may be classed with those of Home, Moses, and Palladino, of showing the extreme difficulty of reaching the finality in conclusion, notwithstanding the time and attention to the investigation of them.[22]

Dr. Crandon was furious when he read Dingwall's cautious testimony. Margery had allowed full access to the researcher and complied with all requests. While she snored asleep in deep trance, she had produced ectoplasm in abundance in red light. Walter had kept his word and made sure the materializations were his best. He helped to materialize fingers that slowly fashioned before Dingwall's eyes-the ectoplasmic hands even picked up objects. "What is wrong with the man," Crandon thought as he read the report. When he finished, Dr. Crandon crossly concluded in a letter to the Society for Psychical: "Research: "using words in a purely Pickwickian sense, to lay down two hypotheses to explain Mr.

Dingwall's treatment of the subject as far as a hypothetical explanation goes.

Hypothesis I: The author is a nut.
Hypothesis II: The author is a nut.[23]

End Notes

1. http://www.pbs.org/wgbh/amex/houdini/sfeature/margery1.html
2. http://psychictruth.info/Medium_Anna_ (Annie)_Eva_Fay_USA.htm
3. *The Secret Life of Houdini,* William Kalush and Larry Sloman, Atria Books, New York, NY, page 450.
4. Ibid., page 482.
5. Ibid., page 482.
6. Ibid., page 488.
7. Ibid., page 488.
8. Ibid., page 488.
9. *Science and Parascience,* Brian Inglis, Hodder and Stoughton, London 1984, page 165.
10. *Margery*, Thomas R. Tietze, Harper and Row, New York, NY, 1973, page 60.
11. *Margery the Medium*, J. Malcolm Bird., Small, Maynard and Company, Boston, page 437.
12. *Margery*, op. cit., page 58.
13. *Margery the Medium*, op. cite. page 439.
14. *Margery the Medium*, op. cit., page 445.
15. *Margery*, op. cit., page 60.
16. http://en.wikipedia.org/wiki/Mina_Crandon
17. *Margery*, op. cit., page 64.
18. *Margery*, op. cit., page 65.
19. *Margery*, op. cit., page 67.
20. Eric J. Dingwall, "A Report on the Series of Sittings with the Medium Margery," page 116.
21. *Margery*, op. cit., pages 70 -71.
22. Eric J. Dingwall, op. cite. page 153.
23. Proceedings of the Society for Psychical Research, 1926-8 xxxvi, 156-8.

Chapter 13

Harvard University Investigates

The important thing is to not stop questioning. Curiosity has its own reason for existing. **Albert Einstein**

After Eric Dingwall's report was published, the Crandons despaired of any unbiased research. "All those psychic researchers can go to Hell," said Margery to her husband. Dr. Crandon took the matter more seriously. The Boston Brahmin believed in the other side of life, as ardently as his Mayflower ancestors sought religious freedom in the New World. With his principles and Margery's reputation at stake, Dr. Crandon was open to another opinion.

Harvard scientists continued to be interested in Margery Crandon, and the university corridors buzzed with stories of her exploits in the séance room. Many at Harvard- student and professors-alike agreed with the late psychologist, William James's to comment, "It is hard to believe, however, that the Creator has really put any big array of phenomena into the world merely to defy and mock our scientific tendencies; so my deeper belief is that we psychical researchers have been too precipitate with our hopes, and that we must expect to mark progress not by quarter-centuries, but by half-centuries or whole centuries."

In 1909, William James published *Expériences d'un Psychiste,* which chronicled the Harvard-educated psychologist's experiments with the Boston medium Leonora Piper (1857-1950). Her mediumship began at age eight, when she heard her deceased aunt say, "Aunt Sara, not dead, but with you still. Later, she studied psychic science under the tutelage of Dr. J. R. Cocke, a blind medical clairvoyant. She developed into an excellent trance medium who gave the names of the deceased along with detailed physical descriptions. At one point, researchers had detectives follow her to be sure she was not gaining information from sources other than spirit guide, Dr. Phinuit. They never found any evidence of wrongdoing.

Other Harvard professors encouraged by William James's interest, in mediums, continued to investigate psychics. For, instance, William

McDougall studied Margery in the fall of 1923. He brought with him two of his graduate students, Harry Helson a doctoral candidate and Gardener Murphy who was studying telepathy at the British Society for Psychical Research. His mentor, Professor McDougall, was the president of the society.

The first investigation began on July 1, 1923. Margery began the session with automatic writing. During the summer, communications were "in good French, bad German, and ideographic Chinese, in Swedish, Dutch, Greek and English." [1] Such communication did not constitute proof to the Harvard researchers, though the other sitters were impressed to receive a message from the other side in a foreign language unknown to the medium.

McDougall was a no-nonsense investigator, well-versed in hypnotism, trance, and hallucination. He focused on physical evidence that could not be fabricated by the imagination of the charming blonde medium. As might be expected, the hard-nosed Scotsman made it a point to keep his opinions to himself and to focus only on the facts. Walter, amused by McDougall's serious demeanor, seemed to take pleasure in startling the skeptic. "Thus when McDougall elected to sit in the cabinet with the entranced Margery, the better to watch her, the cabinet was quietly dismantled around them, the screws being put in a heap in the outside the circle. [2]

Still, McDougall had reservations. He insisted on a thorough search of the house and had every hallway and closet inspected for trap doors and false walls. He even had the servants locked out of the house. The doors were then sealed with wax to make certain no one gained entrance during the séance.[3] McDougall reluctantly agreed to Walter's request for a red light. The dictatorial spirit insisted that the red light was only to be flashed, so as not to injure his sister in trance. While spirit control is absolutely necessary in the séance room, this made for a less than scientific séance-which detracted from the medium's credibility.

Physical phenomena abounded at the séances. Raps were heard from every corner of the room. At time, a profusion of lights appeared out of nowhere. Tables tipped, and the trumpet levitated during séances. Walter loved to whistle and give commands in his distinctive voice. While scientists scrutinized all of the phenomena to rule out fraud, sitters were in awe of the psychic events. At one séance, a piano stool had literally danced to the Victrola music and traveled eight feet to everyone's delight.

Following this séance, one of McDougall's assistant, Harry Helson, found a piece of string about eight inches in length. When he turned the "evidence" into his boss, Professor McDougall declared, "We've finally got her!" "He summoned Margery into his office and told her that they had caught her out at last: the movement of the objects in the séances, they now knew, had been committed by attaching string to them, which an accomplished could tug through a ventilator in the wall."[4] Margery laughed at the suggestions-the ventilator had been blocked up for years!

Professor McDougall was no longer interested in Margery's séance phenomena; however, others at Harvard were paying close attention. In 1925, Harvard graduates, Hudson Hoagland and S. Foster Damon, contacted the Crandons regarding further experiments. While enthusiastic, the two men were amateur investigators. Their findings not have been taken seriously by the scientific community. Nevertheless, Dr. and Mrs. Crandon agreed to meet with the researchers.

The second Harvard investigation began on May 19, 1925 at Emerson Hall at Harvard. Both Crandons agreed to be strip-searched before and after the séance. Control was ideal and the bell box was placed well out of the Crandons' contact. In the next hour, objects were moved by a "psychic hand" and the bell box rang. "Walter was in his element, telling sitters where they could find objects that had been moved, whistling, joking. (He pulled Hoagland's hair vigorously)."[5]

In June, Dr. Edwin G. Boring, Associate Professor of Psychology, at Harvard joined the group. He acknowledged there was a hand moving the objects, but he viewed it as a human hand--not an ectoplasmic extension, "In handling the bell box and other objects on the table, and manipulating and pulling my hair, I was convinced that the "hand" was actually approximately as would a normal hand extended from the medium."[6]

Was Margery cheating? Did the medium somehow manage to free an arm or leg to move the objects or had she somehow concealed an extension as Anna Eva Fay had done on stage? How could either event happen under the perfect control conditions? Margery had even agreed to wear luminous ankle bands to prevent fraud. If one of her feet slipped control, sitter would see this immediately.

Suspicions only increased when investigator, Grant Code, observed one of the bands fall off during the fifth session. Code, a magician, decided to see if he could duplicate Margery's phenomena for fellow researchers, Foster Damon and Hudson Hoagland. Code showed them in private how he could easily slip a band off unnoticed and perform the same phenomena that Margery had done in the séance room. The three decided to insist on Margery wearing bands of adhesive plaster in the next séance.

At the beginning of the sixth session, Walter let the three amateur researchers that he was aware of their scheme. Margery's spirit guide then produced even more evidential phenomena while both Crandons were held under visible control. By the end of the evening, Code, Damon, and Hoagland signed this statement:

(10:16) At Walter's request, Dr. Shapley put a doughnut on the table. There is a silhouetting of fingers all over the doughnut. At Walter's request, Dr. Ousterhout leaned forward and took the doughnut in his hand. He felt fingers holding the doughnut. He said it felt like a cold slimy and rather clammy finger, which felt as if it had bones in it, but too flexible for an ordinary finger.

(10:25) there are now two hands on the table. One hand is well formed. The other hand is a long extension, shaped like a cat's tail. Hoagland feels both the psychic's feet in slippers. Code verifies this.[7]

Grant Code was confused. On one hand, he was fond of Margery and had become her confidant, but he still had doubts about her mediumship. Not knowing what to do, he went to see Margery at 10 Lime Street to discuss his concerns. He told her while was convinced Dr. Crandon was genuine in his belief in the phenomena, he suspected that Margery was cheating--consciously or unconsciously. Code patiently explained to Margery that she had been influenced by her husband's beliefs, and this became a clinical suggestion. "Once Margery had allowed herself to fall into a hypnotic state, it was easy for the suggestion to grow and take shape in the mind. Gradually the personality of Walter developed from this unconscious process."[8]

While this explanation might on the surface seem rational to a Freudian- trained psychologist, it is not a plausible explanation for trance mediumship. When a mediums are in trance, not only do they have different voice and mannerism, they have been scientifically shown to have different body temperatures, pulses, and later voice prints. Naturally, Margery was bewildered by the suggestion that Walter was a figment of her imagination. "You frighten me, Code, but I don't know what to do. I will do something for you that I have never done before. I will give you my word of honor that I have never done any of these things." [9]

What happens next is even stranger. Grant Code requested a talk with Walter who he had just diminished to a delusion of Margery's imagination. During the private sitting with Margery in trance, Code spoke directly to the spirit of her deceased brother. According to the relentless researcher, he discussed his position with Walter and Walter begged him to allow

Margery to cheat ('Don't fail me, Code, Don't fail me.'), so that the innocent Crandons would not be humiliated."[10] Accordingly Code did not control Margery, thus allowing her to produce the phenomena unhindered.

To spare the Crandons further embarrassment, the second Harvard investigation prepared a report advancing the theory that Margery had cheated under hypnosis and therefore had not consciously tried to defraud the group. Of course, the whole theory was ludicrous and it didn't take much for Dr. Crandon and Malcolm Bird to repudiate the Harvard report in their pamphlet

"Margery, Harvard, Veritas." The transcripts of the séances spoke for themselves. As for the private séance with Walter, on which the Harvard report based its conclusion, according to medium Margery, it never took place. [11] Code was further discredited when Malcolm Bird discovered that Code had in fact cheated himself. When the zealous investigator had told his colleagues that he could duplicate Margery's ringing of the bell box, he had neglected to tell them how. "Code had abstracted a box used by the committee to test her, and had incorporated in it, a trick wiring which allowed him to ring the bell by touching externally two particular screws which were in appearance merely part of the structure of the box." [12]

It seems that Grant Code would use any means possible to discredit Margery. He even proposed a theory that Dr. Crandon had surgically altered his wife's female anatomy with a slight surgical enlargement of the mouth of the uterus to make it a "more convenient receptacle."[13] The second Harvard investigation, largely managed by amateur researcher, Grant Code, was even more of a fiasco than the first Harvard enquiry directed by Professor William McDougal.

End Notes

1. *Margery*, Thomas R. Tietze, Harper and Row, New York, NY, 1973, page 28.
2. J. Malcolm Bird, "Our Psychic Investigation," *Scientific American*, 1923, page 129.
3. *Margery the Medium*, op. cit, 404-405.
4. *Margery*, op.cit., page 30.
5. *Science and Parascience*, op. cit., page 177.
6. Ibid., page 178.
7. Ibid., page 179-180.
8. *Margery*, op. cite. page 84.
9. Grant Code, Hudson Hoagland, Everard Fielding, "Concerning Mr. Fielding's Review of Mr. Hudson Hoagland's 'Report on Sittings with Margery'", page 429.
10. *Science and Parascience*, op. cit., page 180.
11. Ibid., pages 182-3.
12. Ibid., page 183.
13. Ibid., page 186.

Chapter 14

American Society for Psychic Research, Part I

Most people say that it is the intellect which makes a great scientist. They are wrong: it is character. **Albert Einstein**

After the Harvard debacle, the Crandons held little hope for academic research. Who could blame them? Margery Crandon, a trance medium like Edgar Cayce, had submitted to every kind of experiment scientists could conjure up. Unlike Cayce who had called it quits after his first researcher removed a toe nail to assess the Sleeping Prophet's level of trance, Margery persevered without complaint.

Her staunchest supporters--guide Walter, Dr. Crandon, and Malcolm Bird- remained close at hand. "Birdie is always willing to try any experiment-with me as the guinea pig" Margery thought. He seemed to delight in meticulously following Walter's instruction on anything from the cabinet to paraffin gloves. Margery had been taken by the sight of the tall, boyish editor who sported a mass of unruly brown hair and wire-rimmed glasses when she and her husband picked him up at the Back Bay Train Station in the late summer of 1924. Bird had a sense of humor to match Margery's own. The two soon became fast friends. Some even said they were too friendly. The rumors made Margery laugh--"Birdie is not my type!"

One thing Margery did admire about Birdie was his unabashed enthusiasm for physical phenomena- and his loyalty. He made a good case for her before the American Society for Psychical Research, when he patiently explained how the trumpet floated through the air. To make his point, he described the trumpet phenomena of November 23 1924: "The lighted megaphone was lifted from Margery's right three times, and lifted to the level of her and back, during double control of her and F.H (Friend Husband)."[1] What happened next was even more astounding. The megaphone moved rapidly out of the cabinet and beat a "long tattoo" on the spirit cabinet. Walter obviously wanted to get the group's attention!

Not satisfied, Walter asked that the trumpet after a few more maneuvers came to a stop in front of the medium's chair and finished the evening's performance by beating a "violent tattoo" against Margery's chair.[2] Malcolm Bird, who had witnessed scores of such levitations, urged the American Society for Psychical Research to stop trying to prove Margery's mediumship which was a matter of individual judgment and focus instead on the physics of the séance room. All the physical phenomena--the levitation of the trumpet, tables, and the ringing of the bell box--could be verified objectively. Thus, Bird ended his official report: "On every ground, it seems best to confine my future work with Margery to the scientific aspects and for the Society to abandon the task of proving here and now, to the man in the street whether the mediumship was valid or not."

The American Society for Psychical Research obliged, and invited Dr. Henry Clay McComas to join the staff on Bird's recommendation. The Princeton professor, was told by the staff of the Society, "All we want is an honest study of the facts." The professor readily agreed and set out for 10 Lime Street. He was pleasantly surprised by the sight of a "very attractive blonde with a charming expression and an excellent figure" when the Crandon's Japanese butler, Noukouchi, opened the door. At dinner, Dr. McComas found each Crandon amusing. Dr. Crandon had a dry wit, and Margery could always be counted on for her madcap sense of fun.

After dinner, Dr. Crandon gave his talk on teleplasm. He explained how Margery was unique in her ability to produce long strips of ectoplasm emanating from all her orifices. He explained that the cloudy substance very sensitive to light, so only a red light was allowed in the séance room. Parapsychology researchers, such as Sir Arthur Conan Doyle, knew well the peril of a light on ectoplasm. In *The History of Spiritualism, Volume II*, Conan Doyle described how a medium suffered "near hemorrhage" when a sitter shone a flashlight on her. Naturally, Dr. Crandon warned the sitters, "We can have no light other than the red light. Please gentlemen, under no circumstances can you touch the ectoplasm--to do so would have grave consequences for Margery." Satisfied that everyone understood the rules, Dr. Crandon then introduced Dr. McComas to the members of the advanced circle, Dr. Mark Richardson, Dr. Edison Brown, and Judge Hill.

The séance that followed captured the Princeton psychologist's total attention. "Margery, fastened securely with a glass cabinet with wire about her wrists, feet, and ankles, went into trance. Walter took over and a basket was placed at Margery's feet. The basket had been daubed with luminous paint, and now all the sitters would see it rise slowly off the floor, then fly back within the cabinet." Walter explained that the ectoplasmic terminal had caught it up."[3] Next, a box filled with wooden letters was placed inside the cabinet. When Walter picked the letter "M", he tossed to McComas. "Here's an M for you, Dr. Mac."[4] McComas could not help but be intrigued by Walter's antics.

He decided to investigate further, and he chose two other professors from Johns Hopkins to be on his committee, Dr. Knight Dunlap (1875-1949), a noted psychologist who had been president of the American Psychological Association in 1922 and Dr. Robert W. Wood (1868–1955), an outstanding experimental physics professor. Both had impeccable academic qualifications. Dr. Knight Dunlap who had received his Ph.D. from Harvard in 1903. He had a reputation in academic circles as an independent thinker, a critic who was not opposed to speaking his mind. On the surface, Dunlap seemed like a good choice; however, his knowledge of parapsychology was limited.

Wood, a professor of experimental physics at Johns Hopkins, also had little knowledge of the séance room, but was keen on research. As a physicist, he was known as a careful researcher. His field of expertise was optics- particularly rays beyond the visible light spectrum that spanned from infrared to ultraviolet. Wood was also a science fiction writer. Perhaps his curiosity was piqued by the possibility that a clairvoyance might be peering into another world that existed the beyond the ultra violet light spectrum. In any event Wood was the first scientist to photograph ultra violet fluorescence.

What professors Dunlap and Wood knew about parapsychology was gleaned solely from conversations with Dr. McComas. Their superficial knowledge of the mechanics of mediumship would later prove to be a fatal flaw. For example, Dr. Wood did not realize how a medium's life hung in the balance as she was connected to the other side by an ectoplasmic cord. Any abrupt sensation--such as bright light or touching the entranced medium or cords uninvited could cause the ectoplasm to snap back into the medium.

Wood was oblivious to the dangers of physical mediumship, so he did not take seriously Walter's stipulation that no one was to touch Margery in trance or touch the ectoplasm. He naive about ectoplasm, and did not realize that rough handling of the substance could cause a deadly hemorrhage. Later, when Wood was invited to touch the ectoplasm, he actually squeezed the mass as hard as he could-without regard to the consequences Margery:

The séance began with Walter who referred to the three professors as a bunch of stiffs, and asked that the luminous doughnut be placed on the table in front of the entranced Margery. Then according to Dr. McComas's notes, ectoplasm was observed around the doughnut with "rod-like structures" seemed to vibrate up and up:

> Dr. McComas: 10:36 luminous doughnut is placed on the tableland between myself and doughnut appears a dark rod-like structure, which waves up and down.
>
> Dr. McComas: 10:27 Walter's voice: "Hold your horses, I will show you in a moment."
>
> Dr. McComas: 10:38 The rod-like structure is lying right across the doughnut.
>
> Dr. McComas requested Walter that it bend to a right angle.
>
> Psyche (Margery Crandon) twisting and withering as the rod moved.[5]

During the next fourteen minutes the ectoplasmic or teleplasmic rod brushed against Wood's hand and Dunlap's head and hand. It seemed to have its own volition. "Jesus, Mary, and Joseph," thought the exasperated researcher, "how does she do it?" Not one to give up easily, Dr. Wood thought "it is probably a leather rod, I am sure of it!" Then the curious investigator did the unthinkable--he reached out and boldly squeezed the teleplasmic rod:

> Dr. Wood 10:52 "My hand was on the table holding the luminous doughnut teleplasmic rod fell into the palm of my hand, feeling like a rigid rod covered with soft leather. It was placed between my thumb and finger which were holding the

doughnut. I squeezed it very hard which produced no ill effect. The rod then slipped through the doughnut and was raised in the air. [6]

Dr. Crandon was furious with Dr. Wood's careless handling of the ectoplasm. "What a cad! He was so rough with the teleplasm, he's made Psyche ill, "thought Crandon, as he watched in dismay as his pale wife scurried to the bathroom with her hand covering her mouth.

In the end, Dr. Dunlap turned out to be as biased as Dr. Wood. In 1925, Professor Dunlap declared all physical mediums were frauds. "With such biased researcher, how could any intelligent investigation occur?" thought Dr. Crandon. It was obvious to him that the two were totally biased against Margery. He could only wonder why McComas chose the men. "It certainly wasn't due to their experience in psychic research, Dr. Crandon fumed. His suspicions of Professor Wood's lack of character were further confirmed when Wood appeared intoxicated at their next meeting. Disgusted, Crandon, called off the investigation.

McComas, who was as baffled by Margery's mediumship as Harry Houdini, attempted again and again to gain access to her. When this failed, he followed Houdini's approach, and tried to discredit Margery Crandon by duplicating her mediumship. When McComas and crew put together his own version of a séance. They rigged a bell box, and used a flash-light to produce psychic lights. One of the men even threw his voice to simulate Walter. It was as calculated as Houdini's stage performance. With little regard to the possibility of genuine mediumship, they men chose to reduce Margery's mediumship to parlor tricks. While he could ring a bell or lift a trumpet with well-placed wires, McComas did not at any time attempt to explain how psychic lights and levitation occurred without the aid of these devices.

However this did not stop these scientists from drawing their own conclusions. When McComas, Wood and Dunlap presented their investigation in a letter to A.S.P.R Committee dated April 18 1927, they summarized their findings as follows: "In view of the above findings, the Committee submits that Margery's mediumship is a clever and entertaining performance, but unworthy of any serious consideration of your Society." [7]

The Medium Who Baffled Houdini

Furious at the charges against his wife, Dr. Crandon barred McComas, Dunlap, and Wood from his home. However, he did not go as far as to deny entrance to the A.S.P.R. trustees, Joseph DeWykoff and Daniel Day Walton. When the two visited on July 1, 1926, they brought Joseph B. Rhine, and his wife Louisa up to the fourth floor séance room. The Rhines were studying at Harvard University at the time. Dr. Prince of the Boston Society for Psychical Research was their mentor. Joseph B. Rhine (1895 – 1980) was sincere in his interest and later established the parapsychology lab at Duke University.

However, the Rhines were also skeptical of Margery. After only one evening in Margery's séance room, they accused her of "brazen trickery" They were particularly upset with the collar control as they felt that Margery's neck had not been securely fastened to the back of the cabinet. Hence, it might be possible for her to produce phenomena fraudulently. For example, the mouthpiece of the "Voice Out "machine could have been removed thus Margery could well have thrown her voice to sound like Walter's or duplicate his Whistle. Later Rhine claimed to see "with perfect clarity, the silhouette of Margery's foot against the luminous plaque during the levitation of the megaphone through which Walter often spoke. He saw her foot kicking over the megaphone within the reach of the hand." [8]

Since Margery was known to snore through many séances when she was in the trance state, it would seem impossible that the event occurred as Rhine described it. Could Walter have levitated the megaphone close to Margery thus giving the appearance of the medium picking it up? Did Margery's powers fail her, and a very anxious to please medium decided to feign trance in order to cheat?

Then Rhine ventured his own hypothesis that her husband had "gradually found out that she was deceiving him, but had already begun to enjoy the notoriety it gave him" [9] Apparently the Rhines believed Margery Crandon cheated in the séance room, and although Dr. Cranon knew that his wife was dishonest, he enjoyed the fame, travel, and fanfare too much to put an end to the charade. When the A.S.P.R. refused to publish the unflattering report of Margery Crandon, both Rhines resigned from the Society.

End Notes

1. *Margery the Medium*, J.Malcolm Bird, Small, Maynard and Company, Boston, page 457.
2. Ibid., page 457.
3. Ibid., page 92.
4. Ibid., page 93.
5. *Ghosts I Have Talked With* Henry C. McComas, Williams and Wilkins Co., 1937, pages 133-135.

6. Ibid., pages 133-135.

7. Ibid., 145.
8. *Margery,* op.cit. page 109.
9. Ibid. page 112.

Chapter 15

Case For and Against Psychical Belief

When I tell the truth, it is not for the sake of convincing those who do not know it, but for the sake of defending those that do. **William Blake**

Critics Joseph Rhine and Louisa Rhine, along with Harry Houdini only made Dr. Crandon more determined to defend his wife. He was not one to give up easily--especially if he believed he was right. "Surely other men of science will come to their senses and embrace the concept of life after death," he thought. As for Margery, she was game for anything especially if only to placate her husband. As she cheerfully pointed out "In the old days, I would be hung as a witch-now I am being researched."

Dr. Crandon was less tolerant. In fact, he was livid when he read of Houdini's exploits. The magician's crusade against Margery had become an expose of all mediums. He even challenged medium, John Slater (861-1932). The American clairvoyant was famous for his "remarkable demonstrations of reading sealed letters and giving names, data, and specific information on deceased people from the platform"[1]. Houdini and his group had attended Slater's performance at Carnegie Hall in New York City. Bess wrote two questions for the medium, "Will my trip to California be successful, and does my sweetheart love me?" When Slater answered "Your trip to California will be successful and will be your first trip to California." [2]He was only half right, as Bess had visited California on several occasions. The medium then added "My guide said your sweetheart is not quite as in love with you as you are with him." At the last remark, "there was a series of giggles from Houdini's "gang" in the gallery"[2]

"Something has to be done to stop this menace." thought Dr. Crandon. With thought in mind, he was delighted to accept an invitation to speak at the Clark University Symposium: "The Case For and the Case Against Psychic Belief." "Why this is the perfect opportunity to set the record straight," a righteous Dr. Crandon told his wife as he handed her the letter. "Our friends Sir Oliver Lodge and Sir Arthur Conan Doyle will be there. Surely reason will prevail."

The idea for a seminar had come to Dr. Carl Murchison (1887–1961) during a luncheon in the grill room of the Bancroft Hotel in Worcester, Massachusetts. The Clark University psychology professor was dining with Professor McDougall of Harvard University and Harry Houdini. Professor McDougall and Mr. Houdini, were on friendly terms, but disagreed "concerning certain matters that have become of wide social interest because of newspaper emphasis."[3] Murchison suggested they and other noted authorities should argue the entire matter in a public symposium. Both men thought the idea had merit as did the President of Clark University, Worcester, Massachusetts. The date for the symposium was set for November 29 to December 11, 1926.

For once, Dr. Crandon had cause to be optimistic. The lineup of speakers was impressive-- Frederick Bligh Bond, William McDougall, Hans Driesch, Walter Franklin, F. C.S. Schiller, Gardener Murphy, Joseph Jastrow, and Harry Houdini. It is hard to imagine a more stellar panel of experts.

One of the most respected was Sir Oliver Lodge Lodge (1851-1940), a physicist and author of the best-seller, Raymond or *Life and Death* (1916). He had come into the field after communication from his son, Raymond, who was killed in World War I: "On September 17, 1915, the War Office notified Sir Oliver and Lady Lodge that their son, Raymond, had been killed in action on September 14, 1915. On September 25, 1915, Lady Lodge had a sitting with the renowned medium, Gladys Osborne Leonard. Raymond communicated and sent this message: 'Tell Father I have met some friends of his.' On asking their names, Frederick Myers was mentioned."[4] Over the years, Lodge would pen several other books on surviving death including *I Believe in Personal Immortality*, 1928; *The Reality of a Spiritual World*, 1930; and Conviction *of Survival*, 1930. As a believer, Sir Oliver Lodge argued "We must not lose ourselves in hypothesis, but must be guided by the facts."[53]

Sir Arthur Conan Doyle concurred. While he was unable to attend the symposium, he submitted a paper, "Psychic Questions As I See It" He believed the key to validating physical mediumship lay in ectoplasm: "If anyone doubts that its (ectoplasm's) existence has been clearly established, let me remind him that three years ago, Dr. Schrenk-Notzing demonstrated ectoplasm to one hundred picked observers which included professors from Jena, Giessen, Heidelberg, Munich, Tubingen, Upsala, Frieberg, Basle and other universities, together with a consort of famous physicians, neurologists and servants of every sorts. The assembly endorsed the fact that they had seen beyond doubt final proof of the existence of ectoplasm.

Researcher Frederick Bligh Bond rested his case on mental communication rather than physical phenomena. An architect, he had received information in dreams and through automatic writing regarding Glastonbury Abbey's renovations in the early 1900s. After being advised by spirit that, "All knowledge is eternal and available to mental sympathy,"[6] Bligh then requested information on the missing features of the Abbey. "There followed a rough drawing showing the extreme east end of the abbey choir, a long rectangular building. A script in monkish Latin followed which stated that this was the Chapel of King Edgar and it was thirty yards in length." [6] In 1909, he received permission to explore the grounds, and found to his satisfaction two angular walls as indicated by the spirit communication. Furthermore, Chapel of Kind Edgar was excavated, it was 87 feet long, close to the 90 feet indicated by the spirit monk.[7]

Now that the Dr. Crandon had the opportunity to be on a committee with men such as Frederick Bligh Bond, he was eager to present his wife's astonishing physical phenomena. However, before going into details of Margery's mediumship, Crandon addressed the most common criticism of her work- the need for dark or red light. He answered "The usual complete answer is these things take place in the dark because of things governing them. One may say 'Why pick on me.?' I did not make the universe of its psychic laws." [8] Crandon went on to explain that the development of a photographic plate teleplays (ectoplasm) may only be created in the dark as light dissolves ectoplasm "A request for quiet and darkness, may sound suspicious," but Dr. Crandon concluded, "it is absolutely necessary."

Next, he patiently outlined the five usual qualities of Margery's mediumship-rigidity of control, the proved independent voice, the great variety of phenomena, the photographs, and the fingerprints. The degree of control was extremely exacting. With precise detail, Dr. Crandon explained how Margery's undergarments and stockings were taped with surgical adhesive tape, their position was marked in blue pencil just in case she move in trance. Then her wrists and ankles were secured with number two picture wire, strong enough to hold 128 pounds to eyebolts in the floor of the cabinet. Then her knees were bound together with adhesive tape from four inches above the knee to four inches below.[9]

Dr. Crandon further explained the painstaking monitoring. "Then the psychic wears besides the garments already described only a searched kimono. Her mouth, ears, and short-cut hair are searched, and the neck is fastened tightly to prevent any movement forward by a leather collar, fastened by a horizontal rope to an eyebolt in the back of the cabinet. She sits on a wooden Windsor chair fastened to the floor of the cabinet."[10]

Under this tight control, Margery had produced a dazzling array of phenomena which was witnessed by the many sitters present. Dr. Crandon listed seventeen separate types of physical activity that included breezes, raps, table-tilting, telekinesis with and without ectoplasmic rods, trance voice, trance writing, musical sounds, perfumes, supernormal lights, various materializations, apports, paraffin gloves and spirit finger prints. While lights, raps, breezes, and table tilting are common demonstrations of spirit, apports and materialization are rarer. Paraffin gloves seem to be a rare and relatively new type of physical phenomena.

One by one, Dr. Crandon described the phenomena. He told the audience of frequent occurrence of breezes and raps. There were also frequent breezes and a drop in temperatures in the room seventy to seventy-four degrees. Also, raps were heard within fifteen feet of Margery: "They may be heard high and low and may even be heard as if made by some metal terminal. Thus apparent communicating raps were heard on a woman's wedding ring. At other times luminous apparatus of the séance room may be seen lifted and used to make raps against the side of the cabinet or elsewhere."[11] Even more amazing the raps came from an intelligent source and would answer questions through a simple yes and no code.

In addition to raps, levitations were common in Margery's séances. To begin with, Margery could tilt and sometimes levitate a seventeen-pound table. Once it had levitated with a 160-pound man sitting on it. Another time, the table had "walked out of the room to the exact location of a piece of jewelry which had been lost for a year or so."[12] Sitters frequently saw the paper doughnuts and small objects, "Many times two small luminous objects such as a doughnut and a basket are in the air at the same time, moving not parallel to each other, and not at the same rate of speed, and they may be seen to be moving in all three possible directions during one levitaion."[13] Next, came the bell box phenomena where spirit fingers would ring the bell box-- sometimes as dictated by the sitter. "In another experiment with the box sitting in red light on the table the bell will ring in 'longs' and 'shorts' in combination of sequences designated by any sitter, the whole experiment from verbal request to examination of the box, carrying on through and ending in good red light." [14]

Crandon continued the lecture with a description of the research by college professors at Harvard. There, under the strictest controls, Walter was able to balance chemical scales. Three to six wooden checkers were put in one pan of the scale. Soon Walter brought the scale to balance as it an equal weight had been placed in the empty pan on the opposite side. Dr. T.R. Tillyrand had described the experiment "as perfect as human ingenuity can devise." [15]

Next, Dr. Crandon detailed the trance writing in languages unknown to Margery-- Latin, Ancient Italian, Modern Italian, French, German, Swedish, Danish, Spanish, and Chinese. While Margery was deep in trance with her eyes closed, one spirit hand wrote: "Qui crea vit te sine te non salvit te sine te"[16]

Other phenomena included musical sounds, supernormal lights and the scent of perfume. The piece de resistance, though, was the materializations visible to all in the room: "In good red light appear hands of normal size, made of teleplays sometimes crude, and sometimes without skin, then with or without fingernails, sometimes with two fingers fused into one, but with two nails." Now that he had his audience rapt attention Dr. Crandon gave more details "These materializations are always connected with the body of the psychic by a cord resembling that which attached the new born infant to his mother."[17]

Dr. Crandon then showed his audience a photo of Margery in which ectoplasm was photographed coming from her right ear. Without a pause, he explained, "It comes from the right ear of the psychic and is pure white, while the, whereas the color of the hands described above are grayish. This head teleplasm is cold, feels wet or clammy, and may develop and spread over the whole head and face of the psychic and pour down into her lap, though it remains connected to the ear of the psychic." [18]

Now Dr. Crandon was ready to present the most tested aspect of Margery's mediumship--her independent voice phenomena. Dr. Mark Richardson devised the Voice Cut Out Machine to ensure validity. Margery passed all tests on this device with excellent results.

Only then was Dr. Crandon ready to discuss the most amazing and hard to fathom aspect of his wife's physical mediumship--the apports that appeared at 10 Lime Street. Much like the mediumship herself, the apports were colorful and varied. Everything from antique jewelry to flowers were transported to the séance room. On one occasion even a live pigeon manifested in the séance room.[19]

Dr. Crandon's final pieces of evidence were the paraffin gloves and fingerprints. The gloves made of wax gave clear physical proof of spirit hands, "The cast of the hand is not that of medium, it is always masculine and may resemble that of one of the sitters. It is needless to say, at the end of the sitting, before anyone moves, every hand is examined for traces of paraffin."[20]

Dr. Crandon ended his case with an appeal to logic: "We know that which appears solid is not so, each atom is a universe of protons and electrons, that of a given solid object, only one millionth part is matter, and the rest is space, comparable to the distance between the stars. Our poor eyes see from red to violet, but we have very definite knowledge of a world beyond the violet. In this field are x-rays and many therapeutic rays, wholly invisible to the human eye. The manifestations of the séance room are childish unless true." [21] After patiently making his case point by point, Dr. Crandon gave his audience one final word of advice. He implored them to maintain an open mind as science was close to proving the afterlife. Solemnly, Dr. Crandon concluded the lecture by stating "'In my father's house are many mansions' has become almost scientific."[22]

End Notes

1. http://www.answers.com/topic/john-slater-parapsychology.
2. *Houdini*, Harold Kellock, Blue Ribbon Books, New York, NY, 1928, page 363.
3. *The Case For and Against Psychical Belief*, Carl Murchison, editor, 1927, Clark University, Northampton, MA.
4. http://www.fst.org/lodge.htm.
5. *The Case For and Against Psychical Belief*, op. cite. page 21.
6. Ibid., page 41.
7. Ibid, page 44.
8. *Ibid., page 81.*
9. *Ibid., page 82.*
10. Ibid.
11. Ibid., page 83.
12. Ibid, page 84.
13. Ibid page 85.
14. Ibid., page 93.
15. *Ibid, page 86.*
16. Ibid.
17. Ibid, page 89.
18. Ibid.
17. Ibid, page 89.
19. *Ibid, page 93.*
20. Ibid, page 104.
21. *Ibid, page 107.*

Chapter 16

Margery in Winnipeg, Canada

It is never necessary to replicate an exact and adequately observed fact.
Claude Berard

After the "The Case For and Against Psychical Belief" conference, the Crandons headed north to Winnipeg, Canada. Margery was excited about visiting Canada during the holidays, so she gladly accepted Dr. and Mrs. T. Glen Hamilton's invitation. "It will be swell to be back in Canada where we have some real friends." After all the bickering at the Clark University conference, Dr. Crandon could only nod in assent.

The Hamiltons were new acquaintances in the Crandons ever-expanding circle of friends. The couple met Dr. Hamilton in October, 1925 when he attended one of Margery's séances. As Dr. Hamilton explained, he had been interested in the occult for some time. "In 1918 and 1919, I came in contact for the first time with a number of mediums-more or less developed-- who gave me the privilege of closely studying the phenomena manifesting through various psychic faculties: among such automatism, clairvoyance, thought transference, and telepathy."[1]

Hamilton was not alone in his interest in psychic phenomena. Many other Canadians shared his passion. The Canadian connection with Spiritualism dated back to 1836 when Maggie Fox who was born in Bath, a town located in eastern Ontario. Later, the Fox family moved to Hydesville, New York, where the famous spirit rapping that started Spiritualism began in 1848. Canadians were soon as interested in physical phenomena as their neighbor to the south. At first, Canadian Spiritualist groups were local investigative societies rather than churches. During World War I, with the influence of British Spiritualism a number of Canadian Spiritualist churches were established.

By the 1920s, Canadian churches welcomed noted American medium such as Etta Wriedt (1859-1942) who was as generous as Margery Crandon, charging only a fee of one dollar for a sitting if spirit contact was successful. Unlike Margery who went into trance and used a cabinet for direct voice mediumship, Etta Wriedt remained alert and never sat in a cabinet. Yet, spirit voices came through and on occasion Dutch, French, Spanish, Norwegian, and Arabic were heard with the help of the medium's guide, Dr. John Sharp, an- eighteenth century apothecary farmer from Indiana.

Sometimes Wriedt even joined in conversation with the spirits. William F. Barrett, a noted psychic researcher, heard voices simultaneously with Wriedt. "Professor Henry Sidgwick" came through:"Mrs. Wriedt doubtless had heard his name, but he died before she visited England, and I doubt if she, or many others who knew him by name, were aware that he stammered badly. So I asked the voice 'Are you all right now?' not referring to his stammering. Immediately the voice replied 'You mean the impediment in my speech, but I do not stutter now."[2]

Another frequent visitor to Canada was the Lily Dale medium, William Cartheuser. The shy Pennsylvania auto mechanic seemed like an unlikely candidate to become a medium, however, in trance he proved an excellent trumpet medium bringing through distinct voices of spirit loved ones, American Indians, and learned doctors. In 1927, Cartheuser, was invited to St. Catharine, Ontario, by Rev. Fred J.T. Maines and Jenny Pincock A year later ,when Pincock 's husband, Robert Newton, died, he made contact with his widow through medium Cartheuser. Pincock described proof of her husband's survival in her book, *Trails of Truth,* published in 1930.

Noted psychic researchers, Malcolm Bird and Hungarian psychiatrist, Dr. Nandor Fodor (1895-1964) also investigated William Cartheuser's mediumship. Bird attended séances that Cartheuser gave in October 1926 to the American Society for Psychical Research. Bird was impressed until he took time to research the guides that came through Cartheuser's séance. The researcher was disappointed to find one purported guide had indeed been a living person. Later Hereward Carrington investigated the trumpet medium, but he too concluded that "a high percentage of fraud enters into the production of Cartheuser's physical phenomena."[3]

Dr. Nandor Fodor, on the other hand, was very impressed by a Cartheuser séance where he received a moving direct voice message from his deceased father-- his "first encounter with the dead." As a young reporter for the "American Hungarian People's Voice," Fodor's interest in psychic phenomena was encouraged by an interview with Hereward Carrington and a later session with Dr. Sandor Ferenzci: "In 1926, while still a reporter in New York, Fodor also interviewed Sandor Ferenczi, leading psychoanalyst and associate of Freud. Although psychoanalysis was nominally unsympathetic to the occult, Ferenczi and even Freud himself were secretly sympathetic to certain psychical phenomena."[4] Fodor attended a Cartheuser Séance the following year: "at the house of medium Arthur Ford in New York. Fodor noted that although Cartheuser had a harelip, there was no impediment in the voices manifesting during a trumpet séance." [5] Eventually William Cartheuser's fame spread to Hollywood where he gave séances for Pola Negri, Jean Harlow's mother, Jean Bello, Walter Pigeon, and Delores Costello. [6]

Less well-known among Canadian mediums was Elizabeth Poole whom Dr. Glen Hamilton designated as Elizabeth M. Hamilton often her as a one of two milestones in his study of mediumship. He believed that his investigation of the medium Elizabeth M over a six-year period, had helped to prepare him for Margery's séance room. The other milestone, of course, was medium, Margery.

Dr. Hamilton first came in contact with Margery Crandon in October, 1925. He stopped in Boston on his way to a surgical convention in Philadelphia with the hope of meeting her. Both Crandons greeted him warmly and insisted on entertaining Hamilton. The two doctors had much in common. Both men were surgeons with scientific minds who were fascinated by psychic research. It wasn't long before the two became fast friends.

Dr. Hamilton was equally delighted with Mrs. Crandon whom he pronounced as "brilliant." "During my stay in Boston I attended all eight sittings and saw under satisfactory control, many of the brilliant phenomena associated with this medium. I witnessed repeatedly successful manipulations of the 'doughnut' apparently by teleplasmic terminals; I observed intermittent ringing of the Scientific American bell box without any visual contact; and as well I saw and felt teleplasmic structures which to my mind were undoubtedly of psychic origin."[7]

He also observed a number of sessions in which Dr. Hamilton heard Walter's voice, while Margery was using Dr. Richardson's Voice Cut Out Machine, which he deemed "absolutely fraud-proof," and effective in proving the independence of Walter's voice.

Dr. Hamilton was so impressed by the séance that he invited the Crandons to visit his laboratory in Winnipeg, Canada, where he had been conducting experiments in mediumship with Elizabeth M. in the twelve- by- ten-foot room on the second floor of his home. The furnishings consisted "of an open wooden cabinet, a deal table (after Crawford's design), wooden chairs, cameras, and flashlight apparatus."[8] The séance dates were set for December 21, 22, and 23.

Margery, as always, was agreeable with controls: "Accompanied by Mrs. Hamilton, she retired to a bedroom where she removed all her clothing, putting on a bathrobe which we (Dr. and Mrs. Hamilton) supplied, and replacing her stockings and slippers after they had been carefully scrutinized."[9] She entered the cabinet, and the circle formed around her. At her right: Dr. Crandon, Dr. N.J. McLean, Dr. J.A. Hamilton, and the medium Elizabeth M. Ten others arranged themselves outside of the inner circle. Next, the gramophone was turned on and the lights turned off.

After everything was in place, Margery began slow, rhythmic breathing. Within three or four minutes, she entered trance. Soon, Walter's distinctive voice came through to greet "the Cannucks" in his usual irreverent manner. When asked about his experiences in Winnipeg when he visited as a youth, Walter replied, "That was a long time back- I was only eighteen at the time. I did stop in Winnipeg, but went on ... Oh Lord, where did I go? Minedosa that's it, I was on a threshing machine, I remember that it was good wheat country." He mentioned he had worked on threshing wheat for $1.25 a day, a long workday of twenty hours out of twenty-four!

The few old-timers present were impressed by Walter's knowledge of wheat threshing with its long hours and $1.25 a day a pay. Then, Walter made mention of another small town, known only to locals, Selkirk. Several nodded in assent--Walter really knew the area![10]

Next, the spirit guide asked for the "doughnut" which was a luminous cardboard ring. With Margery's hand under strict control, the luminous doughnut easily lifted above the table and circled the sitters. Then under red light conditions, the bell box rang several times, showing an independent intelligence at work. With some amusement, Walter picked up two pencils on the floor and tried to place one in Dr. McLean's dinner jacket. But alas, the jacket had no pockets. Walter quipped, "This man has no pockets." [11] Walter ended the first session with a thoughtful question and answer session.

The second sitting took place at the Manitoba Club on the evening of December 22, 1926. After a careful search, Margery entered the cabinet surrounded by Dr. Crandon, Dr. R. J. Blanchard, Dr. A. Gibson, Mr. Isaac Pitblado, Dr. J. D. Adamson, and Dr. R. G. Hamilton with the medium Elizabeth M, and Mr. Hugh Reed, her host for the evening completing the circle. Fifteen others watched with anticipation as Margery entered trance.

They were not disappointed. A jovial Walter came through with his characteristic whistle, chat, and jokes. As one sitter, Miss E. Lawrence recorded, "A psychic light appeared and moved about. Walter said it came from the medium's head. Walter called it his celestial garment. It came first as a small oval shaped body about three inched long. It increased in length gradually to about four feet long and two or three inches wide. It moved constantly through and sometimes laid on the table. Walter said, 'Keep an eye on it. It will look like Moonlight. It is what ghost garments are made of.'"[12] All twenty-three observers watched speechlessly as Walter ended the evening by levitating a fifty-cent piece and by ringing the bell box.

The next evening, December 23rd; Margery Crandon gave her final séance to a most jovial group which came directly from Dr. Crandon's lecture at the Fort Garry Hotel. Eleven people including Dr. and Mrs. Crandon sat in the circle. Walter quickly came through: "Well what do you want me to do; I can't do anything if you do not give me anything to play with." The hostess, Mrs. Pitblado, quickly fetched a glass dinner bell, which was placed on the table. "The bell at once was carried out beyond the table, now to this side, now to that; one could easily determine its position by sound. Often it was heard under the table tapping on the wood. Walter would from time to time joke and chuckle, 'Catch me if you can.'"[13]

After witnessing these three séances and eight other circles at 10 Lime Street, there was no doubt in Dr. Hamilton's mind. Margery was one of the most brilliant mediums in recorded in the history of parapsychology!

End Notes

1. *Margery Mediumship, Part II*, American Society of Psychical Research, New York, 1933, pages 556-557.
2. http://www.answers.com/Etta%20Wriedt.
3. www.answers.com/topic/william-cartheuser
4. http://www.abc-people.com/data/fodor/bio2.htm
5. http://www.answers.com/topic/william-cartheuser.
6. *Psychic Experiences of Famous People,* Sylvan Muldoon, Aries Press, Chicago, IL, and 1947 page 124.
7. *Margery Mediumship, Part II*, op. cit., pages 556-557.
8. Ibid. pages 559.
9. Ibid. pages 560-561.
10. Ibid.
12. Ibid., pages 564.
13. Ibid., pages 566.

Chapter 17
ASPR: Margery Mediumship Part II

This teleplasm is like a bathrobe, a shining garment. Into this people from my side want to come through, if I let them and then the garment molds itself to fit each one's form and thus becomes transfigured into the spirit image. **Walter**

Upon her return to the United States Margery continued as a research subject for the American Society for Psychical Research (A.S.P.R). Members of the A.S.P.R .were as fascinated by Margery Crandon's brilliant psychic abilities as Dr. Glen Hamilton was. From January 1, 1925 to the end of 1929, the A.S.P.R. kept meticulous records of its research on medium Margery.

As for Margery, she rather liked the idea of stumping men of science and she allowed experiment after experiment- as many as their learned minds could conjure. The first volume of the society's made open references to telekinetic phenomena, but did not attempt to explain it. In their second body of research *Margery Mediumship Part II.* It focused on two aspects of Margery's physical mediumship- teleplasm, the equivalent of ectoplasm; and telekinesis, the movement of an object through psychic energy through the physical force that can be from the mind of the medium or from discarnate spirits.

When early researchers, Dr. Gustave Geley and Professor Charles Richet, studied teleplasm, they found that it emanated from the body of the medium. It can take various forms. Sometimes it is like dough, other times like fabric. Sometimes ectoplasm is moist and cold to the touch, but at other times it is dry and rough. Also Madame Bisson and Dr. Schrenck-Notzing who also did research with the following conclusions: teleplasm came from the body of the medium, it shrinks back with light, and when pinched the medium cries out in pain. Other scientists have also tried to describe teleplasm or ectoplasm. Sir William Crookes described ectoplasm as a "luminous cloud;" Alfred Smedley described it as "a cloudy pillar; "and Dr. Crawford described it as "psychic rods " or "spore-like matter."

According to the annals of the A.S.P.R., "When in a mediumistic séance, objects move and the unusual normal causes of such motion, such as lifting by hand, foot or head strings, wires, and levers, magnetism, electricity, wind, gravity, or radioactivity are excluded, such motion is nevertheless, no miracle...Our observation of such telekinetic phenomena in the Margery mediumship leads us to believe that they are all carried on by a material known as teleplasm."[1]

The A.S.P.R. speculated that "psychic rods" were responsible for levitation that took place during Margery Crandon's séance. "Thus when a small basket rolls off the shelf in front of the Psychic and the observer passes his clasped hands through the entire zone between the Psychic and the basket, we believe that the teleplasmic rod from the Psychic's body is either so tenuous that the arm of the observer passed through it without breaking it, or that the rod by some means comes from a fourth direction."[2] The researchers also believed the same rods were present when Margery was able to balance scales with a four to none load. How did Margery Crandon do it was the question on everyone's mind at the Society.

They began by observing the phenomena in an impartial manner, "The mass which comes from the trunk and sometimes from the ears of the Psychic is light brownish grey in color as seen in red light. There is a distinct variety coming from the right ear which is dead white in color like wax, slightly yellow: the color of noodles. Both of these forms are entirely opaque."[3] The scientists further noted that the mass was about forty to forty-two degrees Fahrenheit and a crude ectoplasmic hand weighed about four to six ounces. They were also able to observe that the ectoplasmic hands were attached to the body of the medium by "something resembling an umbilical cord." Sometimes the ectoplasm would from like a muslin clothe over Margery's face; and at other times, the living mass may extend downward in a kind of white sheet until it reaches the table or even the floor."[4]

Walter, Margery's guide took pleasure in producing massive amounts of ectoplasm. He referred to a larger sheet twenty-four by eighty-four inches as my "shining garment."[5] Margery would have been thrilled to see the "garment". However, she was in trance, so she the opportunity to observe the phenomena first-hand. Later, when she read the reports, Margery giggled at the thought of Walter's antics.

Walter was full of mischief on June 6, 1926. According to Dr. Crandon's report, thirteen sitters assemble for a séance that evening. Eight were from the inner circle: Margery Crandon, Dr. Overstreet, Mrs. John Stewart, Dr. Le Roi Crandon, "Monty "Hardwicke, Mr. McCord, Edison Brown, and John Stewart. On the outside of the circle sat J.F. Adler, Mrs. Brown, Dudley, Newman Gray, and Mr. Burns.[6] Walter was full of fun that evening, he levitated a basket up in the cabinet from the floor to Margery's head. As the basket dipped back and forth He quipped, "It's full of energy!"

On July 3, Dr. Crandon reported masses of ectoplasm: "In the old cabinet. Trance came on almost immediately; and before long luminosity appeared in the regions of Psyche's lap and then became faint." Shortly after this Hill said, "Walter what are you doing to me. I feel numb from the collar bone down. Walter laughed at him and said 'I may have a surprise for the Judge. I am now taking stuff out of the Judge, my material which I stored in him some weeks ago'"[8] Observers than saw a light about eight inches in diameter over Judge Hills's abdomen than crossing to Psyche's abdomen . When Judge Hill mentioned that he felt a sensation in his stomach region, Walter quipped, "Yes, that is my naval base where I keep my battle ships and the rest of my armor, I store in the room here." [9]

Walter needed all the energy he could draw from the Judge Hill, Dr. and Mrs. DeWyckoff, Mr. And Mrs. Litzelmann, and Dr. Crandon to fortify Margery, in order to produce masses of ectoplasm: "The luminous material now developed with great rapidity until it reached the top of the cabinet and nearly to the floor, and spread out to De Wyckoff's side until nearly three feet in width. Walter gave us in all, eight views of luminous teleplasm in bright red light."[10]

Walter explained he was preparing for materialization of spirit. In order to accomplish this, masses of ectoplasm are needed so that the discarnate can appear in a recognizable shape: "This teleplasm is like a bathrobe, a shining garment. Into this people from my side want to come through, if I let them and then the garment molds itself to fit each one's form and thus becomes transfigured into the spirit image."[11]

The Medium Who Baffled Houdini

Walter had additional plans for Margery. He wished to make a paraffin mold of the spirit and he would need the full cooperation of the group. In turn, he made it a point to protect the circle from unwanted psychic forces. At one sitting he explained his presence with "I have to be around to protect you people from other visitors." "In addition, Walter advised the group on July 10th, that if they wanted to advance, he would need one year of concentrated work without the general public.[12] He complained the circle was admitting the public too freely, and advised the group to hold no more than one public sitting a week.

Margery knew Walter was right. The demeanor of the participants in the circle had a great effect on the séance. Dr. Crandon had to protect Margery from scientists like Dr. Wood who violated the rules of the séance by his rough handling of the ectoplasm. If any group member had arrived inebriated as Dr. Wood, they were not allowed admittance.

Even though the summer was unusually hot and muggy, the group continued to meet regularly as Walter had advised. On July 15, 1927, the group experimented with the new apparatus called "Butler's little Theatre." "It was a sturdy box with an open front, inside Crandon had placed a pendulum with some scales for Walter to play with, and a device called a 'Sisyphus' which was on a ball-bearing the Walter rolled up an inclined plane with his ethereal powers. During the séance the open face of the toy theatre was encased with glass, providing some assurance that no one was manipulating the objects fraudulently."[13]

The group was keen on using "Butler Little Theatre," and Malcolm Bird was told to place five weights in whichever pan he chose. .He chose to put five checkers in the west pan which was lowered to the ground and remained inert, when the red light was turned on. "The next (display of red light) showed the pans sustained static balance. The east pan was strongly tilted and there was a sharp elbow in one of the suspender threads. Attached to this elbow and running off and down apparently to the lower front east corner of the Theater , Bird saw a thread-like connection.[14] This thread or thread-like structure of ectoplasm caused quite a bit of conversation, before the séance ended. However, when the researchers tried to examine "the thread," it had disappeared.

End Notes

1. *Margery Mediumship, Part II*, American Society of Psychical Research, New York, page 493.
2. Ibid, page 493.
3. Ibid, page 494.
4. Ibid, page 496.
5. Ibid, page 504.
6. Ibid, page 505.
7. Ibid, page 506.
8. Ibid., pages 505-6 .
9. Ibid.
10. Ibid.,
11. Ibid.
12. Ibid...
13 *Margery*, Thomas R. Tietze, Harper and Row, New York, NY, 1973, page 128.
14. Ibid., page 129.

Chapter 18

Psychic Photography

If you prefer blindness, keep your eyes closed. If you prefer deafness keep your ears closed. But; if you are wise, you will open the windows of your soul so that you can become aware of that mighty, vast power of the spirit which will strengthen and encourage you and make you know how life can be lived and enjoyed to the full. **Silver Birch**

The A.S.P.R. turned to photography to capture the controversial ectoplasm produced by Margery Crandon. They used red light to photograph the white milky substance that flowed out of her ears, mouth, and between her legs. One vivid photo shows the medium sitting in a Windsor chair with her eyes closed, and ectoplasm streaming out of her right nostril onto her right shoulder. In the next frame, the viewer can see the ectoplasm flow onto the table. By the last frame, Margery has rested her head on the table in a trance state. An even more revealing photo shows a partially nude Margery with ectoplasm streaming from her vagina. While these images are disturbing at first glance, they do serve as proof that ectoplasm was extruded through all her orifices.

Psychic photography added a new dimension to psychic research. As Spiritualism grew from the 1850s through the 1920s, so did the appearance of spirit faces or "extras" in portraits--cspccially those of believers. One of the first researchers to use psychic photography was physicist William Crookes (1832-1919) who was known for his skillful experiments both in physics and chemistry. "Crookes believed the psychic force to be of extreme scientific importance, and he tried in vain to interest other scientists in investigating with him. He was snubbed by two members of the Royal Society (its full name is the Royal Society of London for Improving Natural Knowledge) who rejected the paper he submitted for publication."[1] In 1874, he photographed the spirit, Katie King, who had been materialized by English medium, Florence Cook. "He was mainly interested in determining whether it was possible for investigators to see both Cook and Katie at the same time, and claims to have done so, even taking a picture of them together. With a battery of five cameras, in his laboratory he took a series of forty-four pictures of Katie."[2]

Five decades later, in 1921, when he had a sitting with English spirit photographer, Ada Deane, Dr. Allerton Cushman obtained a psychic photograph of his daughter who had died the year before. Deane's fame grew when she took a paranormal psychic photograph of deceased World War soldiers on Armistice Day in 1922. "Wide publicity was given in the daily Press to Mrs. Deane's experiment in taking a photograph, on November 11, 1922, during the two minutes silence at the Cenotaph in Whitehall. She was assisted by Miss Estelle Stead. Many spirit faces appeared on the plate. The experiment was repeated three successive years."[3]

Hereward Carrington was so impressed with Ada Deane, that he published his research in the "Journal of the ASPR", May, 1925. "On a visit to Mrs. Deane September 5, 1921, Carrington tested the psychic photographer by willing a shaft of white light to appear on his right shoulder. Sure enough, it showed up in the photograph. Later, he commented "I am inclined to regard these results with considerable interest for two reasons. In the first place, if these plates had been 'doctored' by Mrs. Deane in her own home, before the sitting, she would almost certainly have imprinted faces upon the plates instead of these bizarre lights, it seems to me."[4] The second reason for Carrington's approval was Ada Deane's evidential spirit photo of Dr. Allerton Cushman's daughter.

Dr. Crandon and Margery also admired Mrs. Deane's spirit photography, and sat for their first psychic photograph on December 12, 1924 at the Stead Psychic Center in England. According to Dr. Crandon, "With no introductory conversation of significance between us, I saw Mrs. Deane take two plates outs of her own package of quarter-size plates, specially wrapped in her dark room, and put them in the obviously empty plate holder. I examined the camera, handed her the holder and saw her put it in the camera. She focused first on Margery and then on me. An exposure of each of us was made; then we went with her into the dark room and saw the plates developed; I having when the plates were first put in the holder written the time and the date on each."[5]

When the plates were developed two extras--a young man and another half face- appeared on Dr. Crandon's which he was unable to recognize. On Margery's plate, there were also two extras-- the one nearer Margery resembled her late brother, Walter. It showed Walter with his hair characteristically parted on the left and his asymmetrical smile similar to his sister. The most unusual facial feature-a scar on his left eyebrow- also appeared in the Hope photograph: "Walter carried a scar on his left eyebrow where he had been kicked by a horse, and under a little magnification, the extraneous face showed this." [6]

On December 14, the couple made a quick trip to Crew, to visit spirit photographer, William Hope (1863-1933). "His talent for spirit photography first emerged in 1905 when he and a friend took turns photographing the other. In the picture which Hope took there was an "extra"- the image of a figure who was not physically present when the picture was taken, who turned out to be none other than his friend's deceased sister."[7] By 1923 Hope had moved to London and established himself as a spirit photographer. A carpenter by trade, he only accepted a modest fee- the equivalent of his wages- for his unique photography.

Even so, Hope had his share of critics along with supporters. Researcher, Harry Price accused Hope of tampering with the photographic plates. In 1923, Sir Arthur Conan Doyle wrote The Case for Spirit Photography as a response to Price's charges. William Hope's reputation was as controversial as Margery Crandon's mediumship.

In December, 1923, the Crandons were anxious to learn as much about mediumship as possible during their stay in England, so they booked sessions with William Hope. Margery received an" extra" image that she was not able to immediately identify. When Margery returned to Boston, she showed Hope's photograph to her mother, Mrs. Stinson who became quite emotional claiming the picture to one of her late husband early in life. Apparently the image on the Hope photograph was that of her father early in life. At their session the next day with Hope, two more extras appeared. This time spirit faces appeared in Dr. Crandon's photograph- one he felt "may be my grandmother."[8]

As a result of their sitting with William Hope and Ada Deane, both Crandons knew it was possible to photograph spirit under certain conditions, so when the A.S.P.R wished to try their hand at capturing ectoplasm on film in 1925, they were enthusiastic. The A.S.P.R. also observed Walter trying to demonstrate teleplasm in connection with Butler's glass bell box. "Thread-like structures were shown as supports for objects, and as means of actuating devices; the teleplasmic voice mechanism was seen in red light and photographed. Luminous teleplasm seen in the dark was immediacy displayed in the same form and location in red light, and various psychic structures were seen to change form while silhouetted against a luminous background." [9]

When the A.S.P.R. scientists photographed Margery, they noticed that large charges of flash powder caused Margery to react unpleasantly, so the researchers devised a method that would use less flash powder and still give good photographic detail. Their results paid off. On October 27, 1927, a white mass of ectoplasm in the west pan of the scale was caught on film in front of Margery with her head bent down in trance. On closer inspection, the mass was about a quarter of an inch long and the other- east pan of the scale- had a hollowed out mass of ectoplasm resembling an elephant's foot.[10] When no ectoplasm appeared in pictures as in the séance of November 14, both east and west pans remained grounded. The goal of the experiment was for spirit to balance the scales even though one pan loaded with four checkers, while the other pan was empty. In order to do so ectoplasm would have to be present in the empty pan.

Where did the ectoplasm come from? According to Walter, the sitters sometimes supplied the substance. Walter commented during the experiment: "The place is dripping with Judge's (Judge Grey's) ectoplasm. I milked him last night." Judge Grey commented that he had never felt so tired in his life! Besides comments on ectoplasm, Walter also made remarks as the camera flashed such as "that was a damn good one." to everyone's delight other times, the testy spirit would order someone "to get the _____ out of here! "[11]

The A.S.P.R. took Walter's comments seriously and explored ways to improve the flash process using a new igniter on October 28. While Margery did in trance seemed unaffected by the flash Walter was able to maneuver and talk more with the lower flash. The October 28th séance began at 9:15 p. m. Walter's voice could be heard by all present, peppered by a steady stream of comments such as, "Turn on the red light and shoot in two seconds. " By the end of the experiment "a luminous column moved in front of the cabinet near the scales and while not very bright was exceedingly active."[12]

The column of ectoplasm did not move the scales as Walter had hoped, but it did constitute proof of paranormal activity. At various times psychic structure, ectoplasm in the pan, and beams of light were caught on tape. Sometimes sitters found ectoplasm on their fingers: At the close of the January 12, 1928, séance, "Crandon reported that he felt ectoplasm on his fingers, as did Mrs. Richardson and Mrs. Pearson, by contact with Dr. Crandon's hand, and Walter insisted that they must rub it all off on the table. They tried to do so with little success, although Walter insisted that he must get it all, "Otherwise "The kid might have the pip." (Crandon states that the mass on the table was below room temperature and felt sticky like Vaseline." [13] It seems that the ectoplasm drawn from the Margery had to be returned to avoid ill effects on the medium's body.

In the end, Walter remained disappointed with the photographic experiments. However, they provided the A.S.P.R. with some very interesting psychic photographs, which its researchers noted at the conclusion of their report on experiments with psychic photography of medium, Margery Crandon. "Even though the results of these experiments do not measure up to Walter's expectations, they have furnished some very interesting and instructive pictures that indicate that photography may play an important role in future investigation of the characteristics of teleplasmic substance."[14]

End Notes

1. *The Encyclopedia of Ghosts and Spirits*, Rosemary Guilley, Checkmark Books, New York, NY, 2000, page 90.

2. Ibid.
3. http://www.answers.com/topic/ada-emma-deane.
4. http://www.answers.com/topic/ada-emma-deane.
5. *Margery the Medium*, J. Malcolm Bird, Small, Maynard and Company, Boston, pages 139-40.
6. Ibid.
7. *The Encyclopedia of Ghosts and Spirits*, Rosemary Guilley, Checkmark Books, New York, NY, 2000, page 186.8.
8. *Margery the Medium*, op. cit. page 141.
9. *Margery Mediumship, Part II*, American Society of Psychical Research, New York, 1933, pages 699-700.
10 Ibid. pages 700-701.
11. Ibid., page 703.
12. Ibid., page 705.
13. Ibid, page 712.
14. Ibid., page 714.

Chapter 19
Linking Wooden Rings and Cross Correspondences

Miracles do not happen in contradiction to nature, but only in contradiction to that which is known of nature. **Saint Augustine**

The American Society for Psychical Research devoted much of their research from 1926 To 1929 to Margery Crandon's mediumship. One of Margery's talents was automatic writing. She would sit by the fireplace with "a cigarette in one hand, doing automatic writing with the other."[1] Margery on occasion produce script that was written backwards or in "mirror writing." Her guide would write in the form of a mirror images of normal writing, which can only read when placed in front of a mirror.

Perhaps the most evidential work Margery accomplished in her last years of mediumship. Dr. Throgood came up with the idea of proving her miraculous powers by having Walter link two wooden rings together. This is a feat that science deemed impossible. However, the spirit guide claimed he could accomplish the deed. Dr. Throgood brought two wooden rings of different types of wood to a séance with Margery and two other scientists: "When he held up the two rings side by side, and jokingly asked the control (Walter) to link them, they suddenly were joined."[2]

This was not a fluke event. At other séances sturdy rings, made from of different kinds of wood, were linked in Margery's séance. Dr. Richardson, who attended many of these séances, noted that at other séances, sometimes Walter would link the two rings immediately. At other times, there would be a delay. One evening, Walter asked the doctor to examine with his left hand, ring he was holding in his right hand. "When he did so, he discovered a gap of at least an inch. A few minutes later the space had closed."[3]

Margery was always "game" for any tests her researchers devised. Beginning in 1928, investigators devised a series of cross correspondences to validate her psychic phenomena. Researchers, at the end of the 19th

Century, had utilized similar means to be absolutely sure a message that came from the medium, and was not the product of fraud or even mind- reading. For instance, researchers sent a proxy sitter to medium Lenore Piper. The results of proxy sittings for with the Boston medium were astounding. "The detail and variety of messages identifying and reminiscing about some thirty different friends and associates of the lately deceased George Pelham via the entranced Mrs Piper left pioneer researchers like Frederic Myers and Sir Oliver Lodge in little doubt that some discarnate intelligence was at least in part responsible for evidence unlikely to be written off as mind-reading, even from an unknown source."[4]

Another method of investigation involved utilizing multiple mediums with a method of cross correspondence. "A message would be given through a variety of mediums, unknown to each other, and living in different parts of the world. Each would receive one piece of the message transmitted-usually a simple quote such as, "No one stops to kick a dead horse." The mediums might be puzzled by the unusual reference, but if each brought a piece of the obscure quote, it would indicate the intelligence giving the information was that of spirit and not the product of an individual medium. To the scientific mind, these tests would serve as fool-proof evidence that Margery's psychic feats were genuine.

Not that researchers had been lax. Harvard professors had already put the cooperative medium in many uncomfortable situations. Some even wound Margery in enough adhesive tape to make her resemble a mummy. By the late 1920s, two important experimental devices were introduced. The first, a Voice-Cut-Out Machine fashioned by Dr. Mark Richardson, had offered evidence that Walter's voice was independent of the medium. The second was a glass cabinet that resembled a telephone booth. It had small holes on the sides for the hands, which, together with the medium's ankles and neck, were wired to screw eyes- which allowed for no movement and potential fraud.

Even tethered to the glass cabinet, Margery continued to produce phenomena. Walter's voice was heard as a direct voice coming sometimes from behind the glass cage, sometimes from above the table, and sometimes from various parts of the laboratory.

Not only did Margery produce the voice of Walter Stinson, but also his fingerprints. Much excitement was produced in these sittings by a series of thumbprints obtained in wax that experts pronounced to be fraud-proof. They were partially identified with remains found on a razor of the thumbprints of Margery's dead brother, Walter. Researchers obtained his s military razor, and found that these prints matched the mediumistic ones. R. J. Tillyard, the famous Australian entomologist, became convinced of Margery's mediumship when he had a solo in a sitting with Margery on July 13, 1928. According to Tillyard, "Walter "could produce his thumb prints in the dark more quickly than the ordinary man can do them in light." [5] Furthermore, Tillyard was absolutely sure that Walter was the spirit of the medium's deceased brother. "The personality of 'Walter is shown to be independent of the medium by the possession of a distinct masculine voice and strong whistling powers; these never proceeding from the mouth or larynx of the medium; by his alert mental powers, tendency to impatience, the use of swear words, by a marked sense of humour, a Canadian accent, and many other qualities which cannot fail to produce in a sitter the definite feeling that he is dealing with an independent personality."[5]

Walter was always coming up with new ideas. He decided to try an experiment dealing with cross correspondence. The idea had originated from the spirit of F.W. Meyers. It could eliminate the possibility of telepathy from psychic communications. Alice Johnson of the S.P.R .in London first discovered the idea. She noticed a similarity in messages that were received through various mediums at about the same times in places as far apart as India, New York, and London. "After the death of A. W. Verrall, the eminent Greek scholar and psychical researcher, an intricate Greek mosaic and literary puzzle called the 'Ear of Dionysius' was transmitted as cross-correspondence. In the opinion of Gerald Balfour, and other competent judges, this was one of the most striking evidences of survival yet obtained."[6]

The first cross-correspondence devised by Walter occurred in March 17, 1928, when Margery produced the first Chinese script in red light. She was in trance with closed eyes. Neither she nor any of those present knew Chinese. On March 22, 1928, she produced two columns of Chinese written in total darkness, on specially marked paper. She entered a deep trance and the spirit of her brother, Walter came through quickly with the playful message "All is not Chinese that Chinks." Next, according to the A. S. P. R. "He (Walter) then told us he was providing the energy for the night entertainment, but he was in no way responsible for what the Chinese guests might do or say."[7]

Then Margery's hand took a pencil and in low red light wrote nine columns of script. Walter closed the séance which had begun at 9:00 p.m., and closed at 9:53 P.M. Margery, not feeling tired, decided to write another page. When the group examined the two pages they saw not meaningless marks but Chinese calligraphy-a language neither she nor Walter knew. The script was signed Kung Tze.

On the same date, medium George Valiantine was giving a séance at Dr. Hyslop's house in New York. "During this séance a voice announcing itself as Kung-fu-tze addressed Mrs. Cannon, greeting her in Chinese first and then in English. 'One, two, three, I try.'"[6] When Valiantine came out of trance, he like Margery drew columns of Chinese calligraphy.

Two Chinese scholars were recruited to translate Margery Crandon's calligraphy. Both Huang of China and Dr. Hsieh agreed the calligraphy was "true original Chinese." Dr. Huang worked hard to translate the ancient writing which ended with the admonition "Tse king said the Master's ways were characterized by kindness and gentleness, humbleness, and politeness. Neither should our ways differ from his way."[8]

Walter then announced that he would attempt a Chinese-English cross-correspondence with Henry Hardwicke, of Niagara Falls. Malcolm Bird was asked to choose a sentence that would be given to be given through Hardwicke in Chinese. The sentence that Bird chose was "A rolling stone gathers no moss." When Hardwicke's original script came through the mail, "It showed a Maltese cross within the circle, a rectangle enclosing the name Kung-fu-tze, and the symbols for Bird and Hill, and the Chinese sentence, the general meaning of which was, 'A travelling agitator gathers no gold.'" Johnson's analysis revealed a further important element. In the left hand column are found the words, "I am not dead, Confucius.'"[9] Sarah Litzelmann, from Ogunquit, Maine who also took part in the cross-correspondence received Chinese script- even though she had no knowledge of the language.

The group was essentially experimenting with what Upton Sinclair, the Pulitzer Prize-winning American author, would refer to as a "mental radio." Sinclair delved into telepathy with his wife, Mary Craig Sinclair, who was able to duplicate his drawings telepathically. He claimed that Craig had "over a 75%"[9]

Walter, too, believed it was possible to telepathically transmit. The group sometimes even met without Margery present to telepathically receive and transmit a variety of things--number, sentences, and the face of a watch. In one experiment, Walter impressed the image of the face of a Waltham watch on three mediums. "Like a skilled ringmaster at the circus, Walter then impresses coincidentally the idea of a Waltham watch-like instrument on three different mediums (a) Margery (entranced), eight miles away, (b) Valantine 240 miles away, and (c) Hardwick (entranced) five hundred miles away. In other words, Margery has become like the other two mediums, simply a recipient of impressions. Her impressions are to be sure more accurate than the other two mediums, but they are similar in type."[10]

As Margery's fame grew, the international community in Italy, including Count Piero Bon took an interest in her cross correspondence. On May 27, 1929, the count and others sat in his house in Venice, Italy, at 11 p.m.], while Margery and her followers were gathered at 10 Lime Street. Thus, the two groups were sitting for the experiment at the same time. The purpose of the experiment was to mentally send three numbers chosen at random from a calendar. In order to accomplish this, researchers took three marked calendar sheet s from an envelope sealed by Mr. Bond and placed them in front of Walter. He selected one with the numbers 3-5-10 for the experiment. Later, the two mediums-- Margery Crandon in Boston in white light wrote the exact number 3-5-10. The results were sealed and sent to the Venice group. Meanwhile, in a trance state, medium George Valiantine in Venice received the same numbers-- 3-5-10, and those results were sent to Boston.[11]

On May 29, two psychics in the Venice group received the next group of number in the sealed envelopes. They wrote 429 or 249 at least 18 times. The A. S. P. R. deemed the two experiments a success, "Result attained: Thus it appears that at the first sitting Walter cognized not only the three numbers presented, but the next three in the pack; and was able to transmit the second three to Venice in the absence of Valiantine, and without knowledge by any sitter at either place concerning the nature or entails of this second experiment."[12]

Naturally Margery and Dr. Crandon were most pleased with the results of the A.S.P.R.'s committee's report. These were studies which were conducted under tight control conditions with the nation's leading authorities on psychic research. At the end of the Margery Mediumship Part II, researchers concluded their report on Margery Crandon as follows: "It is respectfully submitted that no critic that hesitates at this logical climax may be any means escape the hypothesis of validity. The facts here chronicled constitute conclusive proof of the existence of Margery's supernormal faculties, and the strongest sort of evidence that these work through the agency of her deceased brother, Walter."[13] Margery smiled contentedly when she read the last sentence. With Dr. Crandon's encouragement, she had added many pages to psychic research.

End Notes

1, Marion Nestor, "The Margery Mediumship--I Was There," Fate Magazine, April 1985, page 80.

2. Ibid, page 85-6.

3. Ibid., page 86.

4. http://www.montaguekeen.com/page46.html
5. *www.woodlandway.org/PDF/19.PSYPIONEERFounded-byLesliePrice.pdf*
6. *www.woodlandway.org/PDF/19.PSYPIONEERFounded-byLesliePrice*
7. *http://www.answers.com/topic/cross-correspondence.*
8. *Margery Mediumship, Part II*, American Society of Psychical Research, New York, 1933, page 811.
9. Ibid., page 815.
10. Ibid., page 817.
11. http://www.answers.com/topic/mina-Crandon
12. http://www.scribd.com/doc/4848575/Upton-Sinclair-Mental-Radio
13. *Margery Mediumship, Part II*, op. cite, pages 786-787.
15. Ibid page 763.
16. Ibid, page 764.
17. Ibid., page 840.

Chapter 20

Backlash

To the S.P.R Good bye to ye- we bid ye farewell.
Walter

Even with such impressive results, the cross- correspondence experiments still came under scrutiny. For instance, when Captain Fife selected the word "Waltham" and a picture of a watch as the target, which Margery correctly perceived, Dr. Mark Richardson attributed the medium's correct drawing of the watch and word "Waltham" to her paranormal ability. To a scientist this fact alone would not be considered proof unless tight controls were in place. No one except Captain Fife would have been allowed in the room to rule out collusion. "However the target had been known to other sitters who were attempting to play the part of investigators. One phone call from any member of the circle could have communicated the target from Boston to New York much more effectively than Walter's psychic powers."[1]

Malcolm Bird remained troubled despite the successful cross-correspondence experiment, and the many psychic photographs. The photographs did not in any way explain the thread he had seen. "Jesus, Mary, and Joseph," thought Malcolm Bird. "What is a thread doing there?"

However, Bird chose to keep his thoughts to himself. Still, Walter (as if reading Birdie's mind) kept cajoling him for even the one mention of the thread. However, Bird knew he had seen something, as Mr. Dudley had even nudged him at the same moment Bird saw the thread. In order to keep peace with Walter and the rest of the group, Bird agreed it was a thread of ectoplasm.

Allowing his negative thoughts to surface was difficult for Margery's champion. No one had done more to promote Margery's mediumship than Malcolm Bird. He was a respected psychic researcher who lectured in the United States and Europe on "My Psychic Investigations," "Fraudulent Mediums I Have Known," and of course, "Margery the

Medium". Bird even traveled to the Sorbonne to present evidence for Margery Crandon's physical mediumship to the International Congress for Psychical Research. He also took time to investigate Europe's celebrated physical medium, Rudi Schneider, whom he accused of trickery "Bird's skepticism about Europe's greatest case of physical mediumship made his favorable estimate of Margery's performances even more impressive. His fidelity to Margery was furthered evidenced as he continued to devote his spare time to the slowly progressing second volume of the Proceedings (of the A.S.P.R.)"[2]

About this time, Margery began to make some concessions to the scientists' insistence on better control and began doing "solus sittings" in which only Margery and the investigator would remain in the séance room. This change, presumably, would rule out any collusion from an accomplice. Researchers also used photography to capture ectoplasm in red light on film.

However, even with these concessions, Malcolm Bird still had concern about aspects of Margery's mediumship at the close of 1928. Bird had initially been impressed with Margery's mediumship and believed that Walter was truly coming in. Yet, he knew Margery was not above cheating when under duress. As Bird explained in a confidential letter to the Board of Trustees of the A. S. P. R, Margery would stoop to fraud rather than a blank séance. "The occasion was one of Houdini's visits to Boston for the purpose of a sitting. ...She sought a private interview with me and tried to get me to agree, in the event that phenomena did not occur, that I would ring the bell-box myself or produce something else that would pass as activity by Walter."[3]

"Was it just a case of the jitters or had Margery been embellishing her mediumship right along? The question that haunted Bird. Few mediums commanded that attention that Margery Crandon attracted. She made headlines wherever she when. The downside, of course, was the tremendous strain on her mind and body. There was no way she could be at her best for every sitting. Add Harry Houdini to the audience, and even a medium of Margery's caliber might be tempted to deceive.

Bird knew that it was not unusual for a medium to cheat. "There was huge public interest in séances and mediums. The shock of the scale of the slaughter of the first War, the awful personal losses suffered, the dwindling faith in the traditional teachings of the church; the rise in interest in mysticism. Death was in the zeitgeist. Until Harry Price's pioneering work, few people were aware of how easy it was to fake evidence of the afterlife."[4]

Malcolm Bird did not place complete faith in Harry Price. While, Price from all accounts, was knowledgeable, he was often seen as a publicity-seeking ghost hunter, who used both his skills as magician and an aggressive investigator to debunk "fraudulent" mediums. He had even discounted spirit photographer William Hope. "He claimed that Hope used pre-exposed plates in his camera, which he learned by secretly switching the plates the photographer was using with plates of his own."[5] Price had become suspicious when Hope insisted on using his own plates. Hope was furious. The medium used his own plates with the name of the sitter on each plate because he obtained his best psychic photographs when spirit sensitized the plates prior to taking a picture- a practice used by many spirit photographers. If Hope had been given the opportunity to explain this practice, the skeptical Harry Price would have scoffed at such rubbish. However, Sir Arthur Conan Doyle believed in Hope. The staunch Spiritualist even wrote a book, The Case for Spirit Photography in response, to Price's criticism.

One medium who did impress Harry Price was Rudi Schneider who, like Margery, produced ectoplasm, table levitations, and rappings. Initially, Price termed Schneider genuine, but reversed his opinion of the physical medium when he tested Schneider at the S.P.R. Laboratory in1932. The evidence? A grainy photograph that showed Schneider reaching for a table.

Was it a single act of Schneider's desperation- mediums as a rule do not do well under the stress of the laboratory camera - or had he indeed faked all his physical phenomena?

Margery's researchers were also keenly aware of the fraudulent practices that abounded in the 1920s. One common practice, which Malcolm Bird was well aware of, was that of using luminous paint to produce spirit lights. The medium only had to paint the soles of her feet with luminous paint to produce spirit lights, which he mentioned in his letter to the A.S.P.R. "This device (luminous paint on the medium's sole) can always be detected by cleverly chosen tests that would force an upward foot to move. Keating and Carrington reported to me that at times they had positive observations that the technique was being used, and on other occasions, when it was not, the lights so far as they could judge were valid. "[6]

Bird himself admitted to uttering half-truths and omitting pertinent suspicions to protect Margery. He began to cast a cold eye on her. Why would Bird have second thoughts about Margery's mediumship after his glowing report in his book, *Margery the Medium*? In page after page, he documented the medium's excellent trance control; her guide, Walter, as well as the many aspects of psychic phenomena. Apparently the Crandons and Malcolm Bird were no longer on good terms.

What once was a friendship of mutual admiration had soured with time. "Bird it seems was seen in the company of a certain, unnamed 'immoral woman' and had allegedly appeared quite drunk with her at Lime Street. Needless to say the high character of the Crandons did not permit them to admit this woman into their house. No longer was Malcolm Bird welcome at Margery's séances. At that time Malcolm Bird was the president of the A.S.P.R., so friends of the Crandons brought Bird's disrespectful conduct up with his employers."[7]

Bird's response the long letter to the Society dated May, 1930. In December 1930, Malcolm Bird resigned from the society over the medium whom he had defended for the past six years. His departure put the A.S.P.R. in a precarious position, as Margery *Volume II* was in its final stages. Bird was well aware of this fact. In a letter to Dr. Prince dated July 29, 1931, Bird wrote, "They (the Board) are aware that they are suppressing important evidence and they can satisfy their consciences only by making themselves believe that the witness who offers the evidence is unworthy of belief. I shall be neither surprised nor aggrieved by anything they do in this direction, after they have gone to the lengths of trying to make it appear that my frequent Boston trips were the cloak for a series of illicit amours."[8] With all the pathos of a Greek tragedy, the man responsible for Margery's Crandon's fame was now responsible for her downfall.

"Where will all this nonsense with Birdie end," thought Margery. as she shrugged her shoulders. Dr. Crandon was livid. "Bird certainly is no gentleman," thought Crandon. The doctor responded to Bird's attacks by barring the former friend from his wife's séances.

While the Crandons were at liberty to close the séance room door to Malcolm Bird, the A.S.P.R. trustees were obliged to be more tactful. If they wished to publish their 700- page *Margery Mediumship Part II*, it would have to be without Bird's assistance with the final draft. When the book finally was released in 1933, the Crandons were pleased with the volume of research. As for Malcolm Bird, the A.S.P.R. noted diplomatically in the preface: "When Mr. Bird ceased to be Research Officer of the Society, he had prepared considerable material for publication as the second volume of the series. The work was not complete and the Society decided that the method of treatment adopted by Mr. Bird could be improved upon."[9]

The publication of *Margery Mediumship Part II* represented a victory for the Crandons who were as determined as ever to validate Margery's trance mediumship. They had great faith that Margery *Mediumship Part II* put the matter of fraud to rest. Why not? Margery still had many believers. All her regulars who attended the Lime Street séances were still loyal, especially William Buttons, who had taken Bird's place in defending her honor.

Buttons was a wealthy member on the Board of trustees of A.S.P.R. along with her old friend, Dr. Mark Richardson. Sary Litzelmann, a medium herself, also remained true to Margery. Walter, of course, continued to be his sister's loyal guide. In February 1930, he channeled this witty quatrain through Margery:

To the S.P.R.
Good bye to ye- we bid ye farewell.
The clarion calls, the ghost in haste departs.
We will no longer bide within your walls.
We'll view ye from afar, ye S.P.R. [10]

End Notes

1. *Margery*, Thomas R. Tietze, Harper and Row, New York, NY, 1973, page 132.
2. Ibid., page 128.
3. Ibid., page 137.
4. http://www.harryprice.co.uk/Biography/pricebyclarke.htm.
5. Ibid.
6. *Margery*, op. cite. page 138.
7. Ibid. *Margery,* page 141.
8. Ibid. *Margery*, page 141.
9. *Margery Mediumship Part II*, American Society of Psychical Research, New York, 1933, page 491.
10. *Margery,* op. cite, page 151.

Chapter 21

"Spooky Fingerprints"

Miracles do not happen in contradiction to nature, but only in contradiction to that which is known of nature. **Saint Augustine**

Walter may have remained unfazed--even though the schism between members of the A.S.P.R who supported Margery and those who did was growing daily. The president, William H. Button, elected in 1932, stood by Margery at the height of her fame and during its decline. He tried in vain to keep the any dissention from the public. President Button served for anther nine years during which, the Margery case dominated the research of the A.S.P.R., attracting international attention. He was certain that scientific researchers would eventually prove Margery's psychic powers to be genuine.

Margery's guide, Walter, remained true as well. The spirit had done his part by demonstrating physical phenomena as psychic evidence of his presence. In 1926, he introduced spirit finger prints to Margery's circle. Séance after séance included two bowls- one of warm paraffin and one of cold water. Once Walter took over his sister's body, he would make an impression of his thumb or other fingers in the warm wax, which was then plunged into cold water to harden. These early prints were verified by comparing them with prints lifted from an old razor Walter had used when he was alive.

Walter even suggested that all the members of the group have a copy of their fingerprints on file, in case one of them died. This was not a morbid idea to the sitters because they all believed in a hereafter. Then regular members in Margery's circle readily made a pact that if any one were to pass to spirit, they would return to impress their spirit fingertips in wax. What could be more conclusive evidence than this.

The first member of the group to pass over was Charles Stanton Hill. The Boston judge died on September 2, 1930, and six weeks later his spirit appeared in Margery Crandon's séance room. "While the medium's hands were held under strict control a phantom thumb was seen making three imprints. Mr. J. W. Fyfe, a Boston finger-print expert, examined the prints carefully. He found them perfectly identical with the prints made by Judge Hill during his life." [1]

Margery's loyal followers felt vindicated. Walter was brilliant. His fingerprint phenomena continued to grow in ingenuity. Walter brought through the prints of a living person-- Sir Oliver Lodge. "In July, 1931, Walter produced thumb-prints which he declared to be those of Sir Oliver Lodge, who was, at the time, in England, 3,000 miles away. The prints were sent over to England. Mr. Bell, of Scotland Yard, subjected them to a thorough examination and pronounced them identical with the prints of Sir Oliver." [2]

How did Walter do it? He explained that while Lodge was sleeping in England, Walter used Lodge's etheric double to make the prints. Apparently, Lodge's spirit double managed to make an appearance in the séance room and, with some assistance from Walter, made a thumbprint in wax.

"How clever," thought Sir Oliver Lodge. He, along with poet, William Butler Yeats, was very interested in Margery's unique gift. One evening, Yeats was even treated to an unusual display of mediumship when Walter succeeded in interlocking two wooden rings during a séance. Yeats was amazed to see that the rings remained whole and unbroken. Dr. Crandon sent the interlocked rings to Sir Oliver Lodge for independent verification. No one was more disheartened than Lodge when opened the parcel, only to discover that wooden rings lay broken at the bottom, rendering the rings unsuitable for research.

However, eyewitness accounts still exist. According to journalist, Hannen Swaffen, Walter was able to successfully join two wooden rings- one of red mahogany, and the other of white wood. The spirit guide liked to play games with the rings. "Sometimes in the séance room, sitters would see the rings looking as though parts of them had been eaten away. Sometimes Margery saw sawdust lying on the table, and part of the rings missing. Sitters have seen them grow again.[3]

Walter seem to enjoy new tests. He later agreed to try B. K. Thorogood's experiment designed to prove that his voice was indeed independent of that of Margery. "B. K. Thorogood constructed a cubical box consisting of layers of seven different materials, sheathed in copper and soft iron, weighing over a hundred pounds, completely sound-proof, closed and nnected by two wires emerging from the box to a loudspeaker in a distant room. The voice in space which Walter claimed to be his own was asked to speak into the microphone within the box. "[4] Walter's resonant, distinctly masculine voice was heard in the distant room, thus proving that Walter was indeed speaking independent of the medium.

Walter also continued to demonstrate the continuity of life through the production of spirit thumbprints: "On February 16th, 1932, in the presence of Mr. William H. Button, President of the American Society for Psychical Research, he made a thumb print inside a heavy locked box which could not be opened without the fact immediately becoming apparent. Before two scientists and a fingerprint expert he demonstrated the feat again and again."[5] Walter was most determined to prove the reality of physical phenomena to Margery's group which included doctors, prominent businessmen, and sincere seekers of truth...

Margery's circle was ready for any idea Walter cooked up- even far-fetched ones. One evening, for example, he announced to the group, that he would produce the prints of an unborn baby. Since the parents of the baby would be members known to the group, verification of the prints would be easy to obtain. "On March 9th, 1932, he made a print of an infant who would be born in a certain family. Walter succeeded in creating an imprint of a baby's foot. "He gave the names of "Mary Jane" and "Mary and Jane". The baby was born, but, unhappily, family reasons made it impossible to obtain verification." [6]

This setback turned out to be a minor matter, compared with the disturbing news that William Button received a few days later on March 11, 1932. It arrived in a letter from one of Margery's researchers, Mr. E. E. Dudley. For years Dudley had taken finger prints of all Margery's circle to rule out their presence on the wax. However, the zealous detective took it upon himself to include anyone who had contact with the Crandons, which added Margery's dentist to the list to be ruled out as possible fraudulent prints. According to the fingerprint expert, "The 'Walter prints are not those of Walter Stinson, deceased." Dudley went on to explain he found the 'Walter" prints to match those of Margery's dentist, Dr. Caldwell, who in fact had provided the medium with the dental wax.

Button did not place any credence to Dudley's claim. Instead, he tried to discredit the fingerprint expert by refusing to print the article

Dudley wrote concerning the fraudulent finger prints. Privately, Dr. Harold Cummins of the Department of Anatomy of Tulane University was called in for a second opinion. According to Cummins, who knew nothing of the controversy, the Walter prints matched those of Margery's dentist, Dr. Caldwell, who had been given the pseudonym of "Kerwin": "His conclusions were the right and left thumb of "Walter' were identical with those of "Kerwin." He also noted that some of the prints were composites of Kerwins' thumbs and palms of an unknown individual. [7]

The matter would have continued to go unnoticed by the public, if not for Frederick Bligh Bond. "In May of 1935, Bond allowed an editorial to appear stating his now-adverse opinion on Margery Crandon, followed by a summary of Cummins' findings. The statement was published without the customary review of the Publications Committee" [8] William Buttons was furious at Bond's lack of regard for Margery Crandon, as well as Bond over-stepping his authority. While Bond had changed his mind about Margery Crandon's controversial mediumship, the A.S.P.R. president, William Button, was smitten with Margery both as a medium and as a woman.

Button' first response was to have the trustees fire Frederick Bligh Bond. Then he penned an editorial which stated that Margery's physical phenomena was "supernatural". While Bond took the news calmly, he did not change his opinion on Margery. He no longer believed the finger prints to be produced supernaturally. In a letter to Button, he explained he had done his "moral duty without regard to personal consequences." [9]

It wasn't long before the news was leaked to the press. On May 13, 1935 the New York Times carried the headline, "Psychic in a Row on 'Spirit Prints'". The next day, the New York Times reported the words of an angry Bond as he packed up his belongings in his New York:"I have been fired, true enough, but the fight is still on and will come out now in the open... I stand by my position that the Margery thumb print was a trickery."[10]

The A.S.P.R. quickly went on the defensive immediately, and put together a report using 300 photographic plates. Mr. Brockett K. Thorogood, a former Harvard instructor of mechanical engineering was consulted. He came to the following conclusions:

1. There is no evidence of fraud, trickery, or the use of any normal mechanism in connection with the séance production of the Walter fingerprint phenomena.
2. These Walter phenomena are definitely proved by the evidence to be supernormal.
3. Neither of the Walter hands as a whole nor as to any of the component parts is identical with that of any known person or persons."[11]

Even though the A.S. P.R. defended Margery, outsiders wondered if she could have faked the prints. How could this be? According to experts at Scotland Yard, a die could have been made and smuggled into the séance room. The London Society for Psychical Research decided to take a second took at one of Margery's fingerprints, which Walter had made for the society. Was the print really Walter's or that of Margery's dentist? "In 1934, the investigation of the London prints, showed Dudley's accusation was well founded; they were the dentist's." [12] It seems that the London séance room was not as fraud-proof as the investigators had claimed. Someone had managed to tamper with the wax- someone the scientists trusted. Only two people would have had the motive- Dr. Lei Roi Crandon and Margery Crandon. Since, Margery was in trance during the séances, suspiciou shifted to Dr. Crandon. Had he decided to aid his wife in the event no spirit prints appeared on the wax?

From the beginning, mediumship had been Dr. Crandon's idea. He constantly encouraged Margery's efforts- lavishing praise when physical phenomena came through. Sadly no medium--even Margery Crandon - is one hundred per-cent perfect. Had there been times when Walter was not successful in creating prints in the wax? Perhaps the resourceful Dr. Crandon had somehow substituted wax with dentist Caldwell's finger prints. Maybe Dr. Crandon, unlike Malcolm Bird, gave in to his Margery's pleas to resort to trickery in the event that genuine physical phenomena did not occur?

End Notes

1. http://www.survivalafterdeath.org.uk/books/fodor/chapter23.htm
2. Ibid.
3. *Great Moments of Mediumship*, Maxine Meilleur, Saturday Night Press Publications, England 2014, page 167.
4. http://www.survivalafterdeath.org.uk/books/fodor/chapter23.htm
5. Ibid.
6. Ibid.
7. *Margery*, Thomas R. Tietze, Harper and Row, New York, NY, 1973, page 161
8. Ibid. page 171
9. Ibid, page 173-4
10. Ibid. page 174-5.
11. http://www.survivalafterdeath.org.uk/books/fodor/chapter23.htm
12. *Science and Parascience*, Hodder and Stoughton, London England, 1984 page 293.

Chapter 22

"You'll Always Be Guessing"

I have seen and I have believed. **Francis Russell**

With all the adverse publicity, is it any wonder Margery Crandon, at times turned to alcohol for relief? Alcohol has been a comfort for mediums since the days of Kate and Maggie Fox, the founders of modern Spiritualism. The Spiritualist movement began on March 31, 1848, when the Fox sisters, ages eleven and thirteen, communicated with the spirit of an itinerant peddler, "Mr. Splitfoot," through spirit raps. As teenagers, they sat for hours rapping out messages from spirit to packed audiences. Maggie Fox retired when she fell in love with noted Artic explorer, Elisha Kent Kane. After Kane's untimely death in 1857, she took to drink.

Her sister, Kate Fox, fared only slightly better. The stronger medium of the two, Kate also demonstrated materialization. In 1861, a wealthy New York banker, Charles Livermore, who had lost his wife, Estelle, the year before, hired Kate to make contact with Estelle. The grief-stricken widower was pleased when Kate not only communicated with Estelle Livermore, but also materialized Estelle's spirit: "The medium retained consciousness while 'Estelle' gradually materialized. She was not recognized until the 43rd sitting when she was illuminated by a psychic light. Later the materialization became more complete, but the figure could not speak except for a few words."[1]

Kate also communicated with the spirit of Benjamin Franklin. Her fame spread to England. In 1871, Kate Fox traveled there and met her future husband, a barrister, Henry Jencken, with whom she had two sons. However, as a young widow, she too drank herself to death and passed to spirit in July 1892 at the age of only 56. Her sister Maggie died penniless, a year later at age 59.

Margery Crandon did not live that long- she died at 53. Her last years were difficult ones. In the 1930s, she began to have some unpleasant spirit contacts. When a European gentleman came for a sitting with her, he left behind the unhappy spirit of his mistress who had committed suicide. The unhappy "Lila Lee" took possession of Margery during a séance. According to Dr. Mark Richardson, "We were trying in every way to calm the troubled spirit when, suddenly Margery arose and before we could prevent her, rushed down the hall, and climbed a ladder to the roof of the house." When Mrs. Richardson followed her, Margery, possessed by the spirit of Lila, shouted, "How dare you come up here!" Sensing Lila/Margery was about the jump from the fourth floor rooftop, Mrs. Richardson said "The Lord's Prayer." Miraculously, Margery returned to her senses.[2]

Not only did mediumship take its toll on Margery, but her husband's health also became a concern. In 1939, Dr. Crandon fell down the stairs that led to the fourth-floor séance room. He died a few weeks later on December 27, 1939 the grieving widow turned to a married William Button, now president of the A.S.P.R. and alcohol for support. The two had been drinking buddies since Margery was in her later forties and Buttons was in his sixties. Needless-to-say, Margery Crandon's last séances were not her finest. By the time writer Francis Russell visited the famous medium in 1940, her beauty and talent had diminished considerably. Russell in his article for "Horizon Magazine," The Witch of Beacon Hill, admits that he had mixed feeling about Margery's mediumship, as he had been influenced by a Harvard English instructor. The acquaintance had initially been very much a believer and had even give Margery Crandon a copy of his book, *River's End* with the inscription: "I have seen and I have believed."[3]

Apparently Margery's admirer later became disillusioned: "At one séance, Margery produced an ectoplasmic hand and we were asked to feel it. As soon as I touched it, I knew it was the hand of a dead person." Realizing, Dr. Crandon, a surgeon, was a more plausible source of the spirit hand than ectoplasm, he lost faith in Margery.

In 1940, Francis Russell, out of curiosity, accepted an invitation to one of Margery's last séances. Age and alcohol had taken their toll. Russell's first impression of Margery was that of "an over-dressed, dumpy little woman, amiable, yet with a faint elusive coarseness that one sensed as soon as she spoke."[4] Dr. Mark Richardson, who introduced Francis Russell to Margery, explained that the séance sitters were attempting to contact Dr. Crandon and if possible get a wax imprint of his fingers. As Francis Russell settled into a comfortable chair in the "homey" séance room, he spotted two photographs prominently displayed- one signed "A. Conan Doyle" and the other "Sir Oliver Lodge."

Soon the group formed a circle and Margery went into a trance state. The sounds of her heavy breathing filled the room. Then from several feet above the medium's head, Russell heard Walter's "ear-cracking whistle. " Walter prefaced the séance with the observation: "Lot of interrupters here, lots of trouble, plenty of them." [6]

Dr. Richardson then introduced the newest sitter, Francis Russell to Walter. "How do you do?" said Russell in the direction of Walter's voice. Walter mimicked Russell, "How do *you* do? I don't think you do very well. Is that a Harvard accent you have?"[5] Apologizing for Walter, Richardson said, "He's often rude." Walter, apparently aware of Russell's ambivalence, did not back down. "That's what the doc thinks"[6] after a few more messages were given, Dr. Richardson asked Walter about the fingerprints. "Not tonight Doc, maybe next time." was Walter's reply [7] When the short séance ended abruptly, Margery hastily returned and invited ever one to tea on Sunday. She seemed anxious for company and support. With her son John, a doctor, now settled in New York with his new wife, also a physician, Margery had little to fill her days. When she was not occupied with séances, she enjoyed spending time with Mr. Button, when he could get away from his family. The two took frequent business trips to New York. Away from the prying eyes of Beacon Hill. Margery and Buttons indulged in drinking binges to the embarrassment of John Crandon who always had mixed feelings about his mother's mediumship stemming from the early days when he was locked in his bedroom during her nightly séances. Even Dr. Richardson was alarmed by Margery's chaotic behavior which he blamed on her drinking. When he urged her to cut back on the alcohol intake, the two old friends became estranged much to Richardson's dismay.

Alcoholism took its final toll on Margery in October 30, 1941. She spent most of the autumn days in bed, with curtains drawn, refusing all help offered from family and friends."[8] On some level, Margery must have sensed her end was near, for she did allow psychic researcher, Dr. Nandor Fodor, a final visit. Believing some of Margery's phenomena to be genuine, the Hungarian psychiatrist asked the despondent medium, "How did you do it?"

"All you psychic researchers can go to hell," the dying medium muttered. Then Margery answered the psychiatrist with a twinkle in her blue eyes and a familiar half smile on her face "Why don't you guess? You'll all be guessing for the rest of your lives."[9]

End Notes

1. http://www.answers.com/topic/the-fox-sisters
2. *Margery*, Thomas R. Tietze, Harper and Row, New York, NY, 1973, page 169.
3. Francis Russell, "The Witch of Lime Street", Horizon *Magazine*, January 1959, page 110
4. Ibid.
5. Ibid.
6. Ibid.
7. Ibid. page 111.
8. *Margery*, Thomas R. Tietze, Harper and Row, New York, NY, 1973, page 185.
9. *Margery*, Thomas R. Tietze, Harper and Row, New York, NY, 1973, page 185. *Margery*, Thomas R. Tietze, Harper and Row, New York, NY, 1973, page 184-5

Index

A

American Society for Psychical Research ix, 5, 6, 48, 49, 97, 98, 114, 119, 131, 147
apports 4, 29, 32, 33, 39, 76, 108, 110

B

Bird, J. Malcolm 4, 22, 27, 35, 36, 43, 50, 68, 70, 80, 89, 96, 130
Bond, Frederick Bligh 106, 107, 148
Boston Society for Psychical Research 3, 102
Brown, Dr. Edison 21
Brown, Kitty 15, 19, 21, 22, 23, 40
Buttons, William 143, 148

C

Carrington, Hereward 2, 3, 25, 29, 30, 38, 40, 42, 43, 45, 47, 49, 51, 62, 64, 71, 85, 114, 115, 126
Cartheuser, William 114, 115
Clark University 105, 106, 111, 113
Code, Grant 94, 95, 96
Colburn, Nettie 8
Collins, Jim 78, 80, 81
Comstock, Dr. Daniel F. 45, 46, 48, 71
Crandon, Dr. Le Roi 4, 10, 74, 75, 81, 121
Crawford, William J. 49
Crookes, Sir William 47, 58, 119
cross-correspondence 133, 134, 137

D

Davenport Brothers 38, 57, 58
Deane, Ada 35, 126, 127
Dingwall, Eric 34, 86, 87, 88, 91
direct voice 15, 16, 31, 48, 76, 114, 132

Doyle, Lady Jean Conan 56
Doyle, Sir Arthur Conan 1, 2, 30, 31, 55, 57, 63, 73, 81, 98, 106, 127

E

ectoplasm 16, 21, 24, 25, 26, 56, 65, 72, 75, 77, 87, 88, 98, 100, 101, 107, 109, 119, 120, 121, 122, 125, 128, 129, 139, 140, 141, 152

F

Fay, Anna Eva 57, 58, 59, 60, 62, 65, 93
Findlay, Arthur 2
Fodor, Dr. Nandor 114, 153
Fox, Kate 30, 47, 151
Fox, Maggie 7, 30, 58, 113, 151

G

Geley, Dr. Gustave 119
Golighter, Kathleen 49

H

Hamilton, Dr. T. Glen 113, 115, 119
Harlow, Professor S. Ralph 23, 26, 42, 43
Harvard University ix, 10, 46, 81, 91, 102, 106
Hill, Judge 99, 121, 146
Holy Bible 45
Home, Daniel Douglas 38
Hope, William 31, 127, 141
Houdini, Bess 54, 55, 83, 105
Houdini, Harry ix, 1, 2, 3, 5, 31, 45, 50, 53, 54, 58, 59, 60, 62, 63, 65, 66, 70, 73, 78, 81, 82, 83, 84, 86, 101, 105, 106, 140

J

James, Dr. William 15, 36, 47, 48, 51, 91

L

Lincoln, Mary Todd 8
Lincoln, President Abraham 15

Litzelmann, Sarah 134
Lodge, Sir Oliver 1, 30, 47, 48, 51, 106, 132, 146, 153
London, Charmian 55
London, Jack 55

M

Massachusetts Institute of Technology 46
materialization 29, 31, 38, 56, 87, 108, 121, 151
McComas, Dr. Henry Clay 98
McDougall, Dr. William 2, 26, 45, 46, 47, 71, 84, 85, 91, 106
Munn, O.D. 65, 70
Myers, W.F. 47, 49, 106, 132

P

Palladino, Eusapia 5, 29, 30, 47, 49
Piper, Lenore 15, 31, 47, 132
Price, Harry 83, 127, 141
Prince, Dr. Walter F. 2
Psychic Photography ix, 125

R

Rhine, Dr. Joseph 105
Richardson, Dr. Mark 99, 110, 132, 139, 143, 152
Richet, Professor Charles 56, 119
Russell, Francis 151, 152, 153, 154

S

Schneider, Rudi 140, 141
Schrenck-Notzing, Albert 56, 87, 119
Scientific American Magazine 33
Sinclair, Upton 135
Sloan, John Campbell 31
spirit cabinet 25, 26, 98
Stinson, Walter 8, 20, 23, 25, 69, 77, 133, 147
Stowe, Harriet Beecher 8

T

table-tipping 5, 7, 8, 20, 24
Thorogood, Brockett K. 148
Tillyard, Dr. Robin J. 133
trumpet mediumship 75, 76, 81

V

Valiantine, George 2, 134, 135

W

Wood, Dr. Robert W. 99
Wriedt, Etta 113, 114

www.ingramcontent.com/pod-product-compliance
Lightning Source LLC
Chambersburg PA
CBHW051759040426
42446CB00007B/437